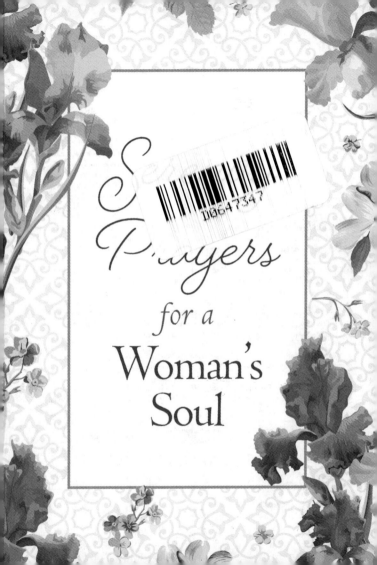

Prayers

for a

Woman's
Soul

Published by Barbour Books, an imprint of Barbour Publishing, Inc., 1810 Barbour Drive, Uhrichsville, Ohio 44683, www.barbourbooks.com

Our mission is to inspire the world with the life-changing message of the Bible.

Member of the
Evangelical Christian
Publishers Association

Printed in the United States of America.

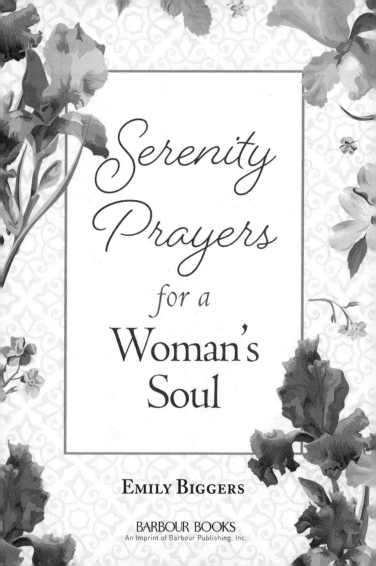

Serenity Prayers

for a
Woman's Soul

EMILY BIGGERS

BARBOUR BOOKS
An Imprint of Barbour Publishing, Inc.

Contents

Introduction

*"God, grant me serenity in my relationships,
my work, my church. . .my life!"*

Serenity Prayers for a Woman's Soul will help you invite refreshing serenity—that comes only through an intimate relationship with the heavenly Father—into every area of your life. Each prayer starter will gently guide you into meaningful, purposeful, honest conversation with your Creator; and the accompanying scripture selections will encourage you to meditate and reflect on God's Word while quieting your heart before entering into His presence in peaceful expectation. Read on, and discover the comfort, healing, and calm your soul is craving.

God, Grant Me Serenity
IN MY IDENTITY

Content with My Appearance

*"Has anyone by fussing in front of the mirror ever gotten taller by
so much as an inch? All this time and money wasted on fashion—
do you think it makes that much difference? Instead of looking at
the fashions, walk out into the fields and look at the wildflowers.
They never primp or shop, but have you ever seen color and
design quite like it? The ten best-dressed men and women
in the country look shabby alongside them."*

MATTHEW 6:27–29 MSG

God, there is such order, yet such creativity in all You have made.
Such beauty. Such precision. Such forethought. There is no way
that this world just appeared. It was designed by You, sovereign
God. You are good. You created the trees in all their splendor, the
mighty oceans white with foam, and the vast array of animal life.
How could I ignore the fact that You also created me so beautifully?
My hair and eyes, that little dimple, my smile. . . Even the parts
of me that I am not so wild about—like those excess freckles and
pounds. You made me who I am, Father. I am Your creation. May I
never waste time complaining about how I look. May I stop trying
to improve upon what You made. Certainly makeup and fashion
are fun to experiment with, but I want to be completely content
with my looks so I can focus on things of greater importance, like
building Your kingdom. In Jesus' name, I pray. Amen.

A Masterpiece Created by God

Thank you for making me so wonderfully complex!
Your workmanship is marvelous—how well I know it.

PSALM 139:14 NLT

Heavenly Father, thank You for making me exactly who I am. You created me and knit me together in my mother's womb. You know me inside and out. I often wish I weren't so complicated. Sometimes my feelings get hurt too easily. . .and I feel like I'm not talented enough at many things. But then I remember that to criticize myself is really an insult to You. You made me, and You created a masterpiece when You did. Humankind is Your greatest creation, Father. We are able to relate to You as our God. Help me to find peace with my identity in You. Even though I may need to gain or lose some weight. . .or get into better shape, help me to accept my body type and to praise You for it. Show Yourself strong in the areas where I know I am weak. This will point me even more clearly to You, Lord. If I could do it all on my own, I wouldn't need You as my sovereign God. I love You, Lord; and I thank You for making me to be me. In Jesus' name, I pray. Amen.

A Daughter of the King

Yet to all who did receive him, to those who believed in his name, he gave the right to become children of God.

JOHN 1:12 NIV

Heavenly Father, thank You for adopting me into Your family. Thank You that I am truly a daughter of the King of kings. You call me Your heir, Your child, Your beloved daughter. I will walk with You all the days of my life. I don't wish to be known for my career or my wealth. I have no desire to be famous or strong or even popular. I want to be known for who I truly am—a believer in Christ—His disciple, His follower, His servant. May I be 100 percent sold out to You. I don't want to be lukewarm in my faith, for You tell us in Your Word that lukewarm Christians mean nothing to You. It would be better for me not to believe at all than to be a halfhearted believer, Father. As Your child, help me to walk in peaceful ways. Make me one who is patient and kind. Give me the ability, I pray, to identify others who need to know You. I want everyone I come in contact with to know what it means to be a child of God. In Jesus' name, I pray. Amen.

My Motives

You may believe you are doing right,
but the LORD judges your reasons.

PROVERBS 21:2 NCV

God, You see my heart. You see more than appearances; You see motives. You are sovereign. . . . You see all and know all. There is no hiding my motives from You. Help me to be true to who I say I am in Christ. May my motives and desires reflect who You are. Just as a child resembles a biological parent, I want to look like You. When others look at me, I want them to see a heart that passionately pursues Christ. I want to be known for being a Christ follower. Inspect my heart, God. I give You full rein. Enter into those private places in my mind that no one else sees. Test me and try me. See if there is any wicked way in me—even the slightest deceit or evil—and root it out. I want no part of it. Even if I believe I am doing right, Father, please provide correction and point out my wrong thinking. I love You, Lord, and I want so very much to look like You so there is no doubt I am a daughter of the King. In Jesus' name, I pray. Amen.

A New Creation

*Therefore, if anyone is in Christ, the new creation
has come: The old has gone, the new is here!*

2 CORINTHIANS 5:17 NIV

Heavenly Father, I thank You for the peace I find in knowing that I am a new creation in Jesus Christ! His death on the cross and my faith in Him have made me a brand-new person with a heart that has been cleansed from all unrighteousness. Though I continue to sin and mess up royally at times, You always stand ready to forgive. When You look at me, You see me through a "Jesus lens"—as righteous and redeemed. You see me not as a hopeless sinner but as a daughter of the King. My identity is not reliant upon this world, my accomplishments, or even what others think of me. You are my audience of one. I want to live today as a new being, one who has passed from death into life through the salvation provided by the blood of my Savior. Walk with me this day, I pray. Help me to please and honor You in all I do and say. Remind me that when I feel defeated, I am more than enough in Your eyes because of the One who gave His all that I might be found sinless and blameless before You. It is in Jesus' name, I pray. Amen.

From Death to Life

*We were therefore buried with him through baptism into death
in order that, just as Christ was raised from the dead through
the glory of the Father, we too may live a new life.*

ROMANS 6:4 NIV

God, I stand amazed that You would choose me as Your own. I
have been buried with Christ in baptism and raised to walk in
newness of life. Just as Nicodemus asked how in the world a man
or woman could be born again, so many are confused about this
miraculous gift of salvation. They don't understand that being born
again is not to enter again into their mother's womb. Certainly an
earthly rebirth is not possible. But our second, spiritual "birth" is
so much grander than our first. A physical birth is a gift; but to
be reborn spiritually is a far greater one. I never have to look back
on that old life of mine again. I am a new creation in Jesus, and I
can walk and talk with Him as my Savior and friend! Just as Jesus
died, my old life has passed away. Just as He rose after three days,
I have been raised as His disciple. Thank You for new life. Thank
You for saving me! In Jesus' name, I pray. Amen.

Set Free

Therefore, there is now no condemnation for those who are in Christ Jesus, because through Christ Jesus the law of the Spirit who gives life has set you free from the law of sin and death.

ROMANS 8:1–2 NIV

Dear Father God, I imagine the slaves who were set free after the Civil War. How strange it must have felt to be imprisoned by a master one minute and set free as an independent human being the next! I have experienced a similar freeing through Christ. I once was bound by sin and darkness. My soul was bound for hell. There was no way I could come before You in all of Your holiness. I was stained with sin so deep and dark that there was no chance for me. But when I invited Jesus into my heart, I was set free. All of my sins were forgiven, and in just a moment's time, I passed from death to life. . .from sin to salvation. My eternity was altered. A joyfully abundant life replaced my sorrowful one. Just as a freed slave can stand a little taller, I can confidently move forward in freedom. I am loosed from the law of sin and death. I refuse to waste my freedom, Lord. I dedicate myself to Your service all the days of my life. Lead and guide me, I pray. In the name of Your precious Son, Jesus, I pray. Amen.

From Darkness to Light

As he neared Damascus on his journey,
suddenly a light from heaven flashed around him.

ACTS 9:3 NIV

God, the story of Saul's conversion always inspires me. Saul was a persecutor of Christians. He was as far from You as anyone could imagine. And yet, You chose him. You shone a bright light down from heaven and appeared to him on the road to Damascus. In that moment, Saul's identity changed drastically. He believed in You, and his life was never again the same. Saul became Paul, the great apostle of the Lord Jesus Christ. He went from murderer to messenger in a flash. He laid down his weapons for the Word of God; he stopped killing and started evangelizing. I pray that others might see a difference in me, the way others saw a change in Saul. I want to be identified as one who walks closely with You, Lord. I want to be known as a bold disciple of Christ. Give me strength all the days of my life to live for You. I may not have seen a bright light, but I have come to know Jesus—and I want to shine for Him in all I do and say. In His name, I pray. Amen.

Living Free

For we know that our old self was crucified with him
so that the body ruled by sin might be done away with,
that we should no longer be slaves to sin.

ROMANS 6:6 NIV

God, the old has gone; the new has come. I am no longer a slave to sin, but I have been set free. Help me to live as one who is free. Just as a dog who has been trained to sleep in a kennel will return to it night after night—even if the cage is not locked once he enters—I tend to wander back to my captivity. I remember what it was like to be a slave to sin. I could not help myself, quite literally. But then You entered my heart, and everything changed. My old self is no longer alive, so I never need to wander back into slavery again. I am free, and I will live as if I am free indeed. Christ in me. Emmanuel. God with us. Remind me, every moment of every day, of the new identity You have blessed me with, Father. Help me to focus on Christ and never look back. There is no need to act as a slave when one has been set free! In Jesus' name, amen.

God, Grant Me Serenity
In My Relationships

Live at Peace

*If it is possible, as far as it depends on you,
live at peace with everyone.*

Romans 12:18 NIV

Heavenly Father, I think the inability to live at peace with others comes down to selfishness. I get so caught up in myself sometimes that I am unable to see the bigger picture. Just because someone hurts me, I don't have to react in anger or retaliation. Just because I disagree, I don't have to argue or tear someone else down in order to promote my opinion. Just because I may be right, I don't have to push my agenda on others. There is a better way. It is the way Jesus showed us when He walked on earth. He came as a servant leader. He loved all people and walked humbly and in a godly manner. He modeled for me what it means to live at peace with people. I know there will be times when I will be called to stand up for You in boldness. I may offend others with my message or the stand I take. But when it is possible, please give me the humility and grace I need in order to live peacefully with those around me. In Jesus' name, I pray. Amen.

Love One Another

"A new command I give you: Love one another. As I have loved you, so you must love one another. By this everyone will know that you are my disciples, if you love one another."

John 13:34–35 NIV

God of love, I come before You now, and I feel ashamed. I am sorry that so many times my words are not spoken in love. My actions are not always a reflection of love either. My heart, at times, is filled with anger or disgust and packed so tightly with these emotions that there is no room left for love. Help me to see my family through Your eyes, Father. Help me to see my coworkers and friends through Your lens of love. Just as You have lavished love upon me, may I in turn love others. I want to be known as a child of God. I want the way I live and breathe and act and serve to reflect Your great love for the world. As I seek to live at peace with others, will You help me to love them well? Give me opportunities to show Your love to those who need it the very most. In Your Son's name—the name of the One who loved us enough to give His very life—I pray. Amen.

Be of One Mind

*Finally, brothers and sisters, rejoice! Strive for full restoration,
encourage one another, be of one mind, live in peace.
And the God of love and peace will be with you.*

2 CORINTHIANS 13:11 NIV

Father, I long for serenity in my relationships. I want to be like-minded with those in my closest circles. Even among my Christian brothers and sisters, there is much disunity. I hear it in the way we gossip at times or tear one another down with snide comments. There are certainly things we disagree on within the church, but we are called to encourage one another. That is so hard to do when we are looking for fault! Before I look for the twig in my brother's or sister's eye, allow me to see the log in my own, Father! May there be a restoration of relationship in the broken places You find in my life. Help me to be a peacemaker, not a wave maker. Give me opportunities to shine for You, and help me to be seen as one who lives at peace with others. Replace my critical eyes and tongue with vision and words straight from Your holy heart. In Jesus' name, I pray. Amen.

Reflecting God's Light

No one has ever seen God; but if we love one another,
God lives in us and his love is made complete in us.

1 JOHN 4:12 NIV

Holy God, no one has ever seen You. You are too holy for us to look upon. And yet, I have seen You in others. I have seen You in teachers in my church who give of themselves tirelessly, serving and spreading Your Word to all who will listen. I have seen You in family members and friends whose hearts reflect compassion. They reach out instead of focusing inward. They reflect Your light in a dark world. Father, I pray that others would see that same light in me. As I work and play with friends and family, I pray that my love for them would be evident. I pray my words and actions would show that Jesus Christ has taken up residence in my heart and that I truly live for Him. I want to point others to You all of my days, Father. Teach me to love as You love. In the name of Jesus, I ask these things. Amen.

Relating to My Parents

"Honor your father and your mother, so that you may live long in the land the LORD your God is giving you."

EXODUS 20:12 NIV

God, please help me to honor my parents. Show me what honoring them means, now that I am a grown woman and they are growing older. I want to honor them in a way that pleases You, but sometimes there is strife in our relationship. I find it hard to balance all the roles I have now. My relationship with my mom and dad was much simpler when I was a child. I was to obey them, and that was that. Now things are different: I don't always make the same decisions for my life that they would choose for me, and yet I want to honor them. Teach me how to listen without being led to annoyance. Show me how to treat my parents with respect, no matter what. They are a blessing to me, chosen by You to be some of the closest people in my life. I love them, Father, and I want to honor You in how I relate to them. May this be a peaceful relationship for all of us. In Jesus' name, I ask it. Amen.

Generosity in Relationships

A generous person will prosper;
whoever refreshes others will be refreshed.

PROVERBS 11:25 NIV

Heavenly Father, show me ways I can be more generous in my relationships. I want to be a safe person for those who are closest in my life. I want to provide a listening ear and a shoulder to cry on when it is needed. I have been blessed with so many resources; help me to give generously when others are in need. I know that, at times, I am too focused on my own problems. I share my latest complaint or concern with anyone who will listen! Calm my spirit, Lord, and help me to see—*truly* see—the needs of those around me. I experience such refreshment in the presence of certain friends. I literally leave my time with them feeling as though I have been in the presence of Jesus. Give me that type of generous and loving spirit so that I might be at peace in all of my relationships. Even more, I pray that I am a blessing to all those with whom I come in contact. In Jesus' name, I pray. Amen.

Be Found Trustworthy

*A gossip betrays a confidence,
but a trustworthy person keeps a secret.*

PROVERBS 11:13 NIV

God, I know that being found trustworthy is of extreme importance. I think of the great men and women of the Bible who were upright and of good character. They were not going around gossiping about others. They were busy about Your work, and they sought You through the reading of Your Word. They came before You in prayer. They focused on You and You alone. Just as the words of the old hymn go: "Turn your eyes upon Jesus. Look full in His wonderful face. And the things of earth will grow strangely dim in the light of His glory and grace." It is so true, Lord. Teach me to concentrate fully on doing Your will. Help me to be found trustworthy, not only by others, but by You, my God. I want to be someone whom others can trust. Help me to avoid idleness and gossip. Neither brings blessing or serenity to my relationships. In Jesus' name, amen.

A Kind Woman

A kindhearted woman gains honor,
but ruthless men gain only wealth.

PROVERBS 11:16 NIV

Kind God, give me a kind heart. Help me to commit random acts of kindness today that will bless my family and friends. When I am busy at work, help me to keep my cool and respond with grace and patience to others' demands. At the end of a long day, give me a gentle spirit as I deal with my family. Help me to listen and to nurture each member of my family with kindness, for I know this pleases You. You will replenish me with Your never-ending grace and love. You will continue to pour love into me so that I will have enough to pour it right back out into the lives of those who look to me as an example. I pray that I will never be known for what I have or what I earn, but rather for the kindness that spills forth from my heart. God, make me kind. In Jesus' name, I ask this. Amen.

Being a Loving Wife

A wife of noble character is her husband's crown,
but a disgraceful wife is like decay in his bones.

PROVERBS 12:4 NIV

Heavenly Father, it's so easy to get caught up in the world's view of marriage. All around me the world says to look for what you can "get" out of a marriage, when I know that You desire us to "give." If I seek to give 50 percent while my husband gives the other half, I will always come up empty. I must be fully present in my marriage, giving 100 percent to my mate. Even if he is not giving fully to me, Lord, help me to keep my vows. May I be quick to encourage my husband. Help me to show him the respect he needs. He looks to me for support, and he needs to know I am always here for him. When instead I begin to focus on his faults, my marriage becomes not the peaceful one I long for it to be. Give me grace for my spouse, just as You are so gracious with me, God. Help me to be patient with him, even as You are patient with me. I long for my marriage to reflect Your eternal love. In Jesus' name, I ask for Your blessing on my marriage. Amen.

Be Still and Know

He says, "Be still, and know that I am God; I will be exalted
among the nations, I will be exalted in the earth."

PSALM 46:10 NIV

Heavenly Father, as I enter into this quiet time with You, I ask that You help me to remember You are still God and You are still in control. Even as politics and culture seem to be going nowhere fast, I will rely upon the one true God. I will find my refuge and my strength in You and in You alone. You are the Great I Am. You are the Alpha and the Omega. Before there was time, You were. If men and women do not praise You, the rocks will have to cry out. You are that holy. You are that supreme. You simply must be praised. Father, help me to seek You and to truly find You in my quiet times. As I still my heart before You and open Your Word, lead me to the right scriptures and the right messages from You. Clear my mind of all the distractions that fight for my attention. Help me to find peaceful moments alone with You, in which You can encourage and strengthen me. I need You so. In Jesus' name, amen.

Near to God

Come near to God and he will come near to you.
Wash your hands, you sinners, and purify
your hearts, you double-minded.

JAMES 4:8 NIV

God, draw near to me, I pray. Just as I long for human touch and connection, I long (even more so) for a connection with You. You are my Creator, my Savior, my very best friend. Your Word tells me that when I draw near to You, You are there. You stand ready. You draw near to me as well. You have put in me a free will. You have given me a choice. I can choose to live life on my own, forgetting You are there, neglecting Your Word, forging my own path. Or I can depend upon You, draw from Your amazing strength, and lean upon You. Father, I would be so foolish to do anything but draw closer and closer to You with each passing day. In times that I begin to stray, reach out to me, Father. Never let me go. Draw me close to You as a mother holds her young. I want to be in the safest place of all—in Your arms. In Jesus' name, amen.

Peace in My Prayers

*"But when you pray, go into your room, close the door and
pray to your Father, who is unseen. Then your Father,
who sees what is done in secret, will reward you."*

MATTHEW 6:6 NIV

God, I come to You in this secret place. I have withdrawn from
the world and all its busyness in order to hear You speak. I seek
You here in private. Just the two of us. I speak words of praise
and thanksgiving. I present requests to You for my own needs
and the needs of others. I ask Your forgiveness for sins—not
just in general, but for specific sins that come to mind as I pray.
I find time to be quiet before You here as well. I do not desire
to do all the talking. This is not a one-way conversation. I want
prayer to be an open line of communication between You, the
sovereign God, and His servant. I cannot see You, Lord, but
I can feel You near me when I pray and when I spend time
in Your Word. Help me to always find such peaceful, quiet
times to withdraw from all the responsibilities of the day and
simply meet with my Father. In Jesus' name, I pray. Amen.

Early in the Morning

*Very early in the morning, while it was
still dark, Jesus got up, left the house and
went off to a solitary place, where he prayed.*

MARK 1:35 NIV

Jesus, You set an example for me. I read in the book of Mark that You went off alone to pray in a solitary place. You went early in the morning. You didn't wait until You fell into bed, exhausted, at the end of a long day. You sought Your heavenly Father in prayer first thing. Before the cock crowed. Before the world woke up. Before the busyness of day-to-day life began. This is the example You set for me, and this is the example I will follow. I will set this example for my children. I want to honor You in all I do, including how I begin my day. As I meet with You here and now, I ask You to calm my spirit. Make this a time of tranquility. Enter into my thoughts, I ask, and guide me with wisdom that comes only from You. Put Your mark upon my day. As I turn to my responsibilities as a wife, mother, employee, and friend, I pray that You will bless my day. Thank You for this peaceful time with You. It is only through You that I can pray. Amen.

Fellowship with God

*"Here I am! I stand at the door and knock. If anyone
hears my voice and opens the door, I will come in
and eat with that person, and they with me."*

REVELATION 3:20 NIV

I am so blessed, Lord, that You have come into my life. You knocked at the door of my heart. I remember that day. I remember life on my own, before I knew You—before You came into my heart and began to walk with me, doing life with me, guiding me in Your ways. Those were not my best days, God. These—with You—are. I have the privilege of fellowshipping with the Creator of the universe. I get to visit with the Great I Am. May I never take this privilege for granted or forget with whom I speak. You set the stars in their places. You know the number of hairs on my head. I am so blessed to be able to call out to You in prayer. It is only by the blood of Jesus that I am able to come before You. As I meet with You, as I sit at Your feet, Lord, I ask that You bring over me a sense of peace and joy. Regardless of outward circumstances, I can always find contentment in You, Father. It is in the name of the Prince of Peace, Jesus, that I pray this prayer. Amen.

Rest in the Lord

Truly my soul finds rest in God;
my salvation comes from him.

PSALM 62:1 NIV

God, this world is busy. We find ways to occupy our every waking minute. Work dominates our days and nights. We busy ourselves with hobbies and meetings and even entertainment. We feel we must exercise and socialize. We work hard and play hard only to fall into bed at the end of long days without acknowledging You at all. Father, You are my only source of true rest. You offer me peace that this world does not know. The world may offer me many things, but peace it cannot give—the world knows nothing of peace. When my head hits the pillow tonight, may I be found faithful. May I seek You even in my rest. May I commit my soul to You even as I sleep. You are my salvation and my joy. You are my strength and my serenity. It is in the name of Your Son, Jesus the Christ, I pray. Amen.

God, Grant Me Serenity
At Work

Faithful Worker

Servants, do what you're told by your earthly masters.
And don't just do the minimum that will get you by. Do your
best. Work from the heart for your real Master, for God, confident
that you'll get paid in full when you come into your inheritance.
Keep in mind always that the ultimate Master you're serving
is Christ. The sullen servant who does shoddy work will be held
responsible. Being a follower of Jesus doesn't cover up bad work.

COLOSSIANS 3:22–25 MSG

God, I admit sometimes I don't give it my all at work. Most of
the time I do. . . . Sometimes I even go overboard, working too
many hours and neglecting other areas of my life. But, at times, I
do get on the internet or waste time in other ways. I am tempted
to gossip with coworkers or belittle my employer in some way. I
am not all that I should be in my workplace. Help me, Father, to
be faithful to You even in my work. I know that when I do my
very best, others around me take notice. You tell me in Your Word
to let my light shine before others so that they will see my good
works and glorify my Father who is in heaven. This means that
my work matters to You. Grant me the ability and desire to work
as if I am working for You every single day. Because, in fact, I am!
You are my ultimate authority, and I want to please You, Father.
I know that when I am faithful in my work, You will show me
favor. In Jesus' name, I pray. Amen.

Work and Rest

By the seventh day God had finished his work. On the seventh day he rested from all his work. God blessed the seventh day. He made it a Holy Day because on that day he rested from his work, all the creating God had done. This is the story of how it all started, of Heaven and Earth when they were created.

GENESIS 2:2–4 MSG

Heavenly Father, I read in Ecclesiastes that there is a time for everything. A time to work and a time to rest. When You created the earth, You set a model for us to follow. You worked and then You rested. Grant me the wisdom in this, Lord. Help me to work hard and to please You in all that I do in the workplace. Help me also to know when it is time to rest. This is tricky, and I need Your wisdom and guidance in order to strike a balance, Lord. My family is important. My friends need some of my time as well. My spirit needs to be renewed by gathering with Your people in church regularly. May I always honor You in my work *and* in my rest. In Jesus' name, I pray. Amen.

Making a Difference in My Work

GOD took the Man and set him down in the Garden
of Eden to work the ground and keep it in order.

GENESIS 2:15 MSG

Father, from the very beginning there has been work. Though my work sometimes feels mundane, help me to discover the meaning in it. Guide me to a greater understanding of all the ways I am making a difference in the world. Give me opportunities to make a kingdom difference in my work, Lord. If there are those with whom You want me to share Christ, make it evident to me. Show me relationships that I need to nurture with certain coworkers so that, over time, I might lead them to know Your Son as their personal Savior too. As I work, give me endurance to accomplish the tasks at hand. Give me peace with my colleagues—those higher than me and those beneath me in rank. May I find favor with my superiors even as Your servant Joseph found favor in Pharaoh's palace. Help me to speak up when I should and to hold my tongue when that is what's best. It is in Jesus' name, I pray for You to guide me in my workplace. Amen.

Housework

She carefully watches everything in her household
and suffers nothing from laziness.

PROVERBS 31:27 NLT

Father God, I just can't imagine that washing dishes and doing laundry can bring You glory! Does driving the carpool and making spaghetti for dinner mean anything to You? Surely not, I would think! But then I read about the Proverbs 31 woman, and I find her busy about household chores. I want to be such a woman, Lord. Show me how to make the most of my time and to be organized in my approach to household tasks. Housework is not necessarily fun, but it is necessary and I want to stay on top of it. I want my home to be a place of refuge and enjoyment for not only my family, but for all who enter its doors. May I be blessed with Your favor as I seek to be the best woman that I can be. I need Your help, Lord, for I admit that working at home often feels so mundane and useless. Make me a faithful worker both inside and outside of my house. In Jesus' name, I pray. Amen.

Wisdom in My Work

She goes to inspect a field and buys it;
with her earnings she plants a vineyard.

PROVERBS 31:16 NLT

Heavenly Father, I am called on to make a lot of decisions in my work. Every day there are choices to be made, and I am not always sure what's best. Give me wisdom, I pray, to make the best decisions. Help me to always consider any ethical and moral implications. Guide me to think about others and to think beyond today and into the future. I read about the wife and mother in Proverbs 31, and I see her going about her work with precision and wisdom. She inspects a field, buys it, and plants a vineyard. She is not frivolous or flighty. She is busy at her work, but she takes time to consider options and she appears to take wise paths. Make me wise and conscientious in all I do in my work. It is in Jesus' name, I pray. Amen.

When Work Feels Useless

*I replied, "But my work seems so useless! I have spent
my strength for nothing and to no purpose. Yet I leave it
all in the LORD's hand; I will trust God for my reward."*

ISAIAH 49:4 NLT

Father God, I am spent. My work wears me out, and it seems—
at least some days—to serve no purpose. I don't always understand
why You have kept me here in this job for so long. It feels like a
dead end. I put in hours and hours, week after week, and for what?
A paycheck that hardly covers the bills. Father, I don't want to
have this poor attitude. Turn me around in my thinking. Remind
me that You have me in this job, at this time in my life, for a
purpose. I may not always be here, but for as long as I am, please
help me to honor You in it. I will choose to leave my questions
at the foot of the throne and accept my position for today. Give
me the grace to do so tomorrow. And show me if and when it is
time for a change. I pray that You will bring just the right people
and job opportunities across my path when it's time for a change.
In Jesus' name, I ask these things, and for Your glory. Amen.

Provision

*A hard worker has plenty of food,
but a person who chases fantasies has no sense.*

PROVERBS 12:11 NLT

Heavenly Father, You have always provided for me. You meet my needs so wonderfully. The Bible says that You even care for the birds of the air, providing the food they need. . .and so how much more will you provide for us—Your children! I thank You for my job that helps to provide money for my family. I ask You to keep me grounded and focused on the work at hand. I have seen what happens when people stray from that focus and get caught up in chasing dreams. While I know You can make dreams come true for me as well, I want to thank You for the day-to-day routine. My family is fed and clothed, and we have shelter over our heads. Your provision of work for me helps to sustain this for my family. Please bless me in my work each day, and help me to honor You with not only my work but my attitude about it as well. In Jesus' name, I pray. Amen.

Avoiding Shortcuts

Good planning and hard work lead to prosperity,
but hasty shortcuts lead to poverty.

PROVERBS 21:5 NLT

God, I've learned the hard way that shortcuts are not all they're cracked up to be! Often, when I try to take the easy way out or the easiest path, things don't turn out so great. I ask that You would help me to be a good planner and a hard worker. Show me the work cut out for me, and help me to accomplish those tasks in a way that pleases You. I know there is blessing in staying organized, focused, and driven. May I honor You in my work, and may I go the extra mile in all I do. Employers notice these things, Father. A good attitude and hard work stand out in the world today. So many people are lazy or trying to find a way to make more money by doing less work. Even if it never gets me ahead or helps me climb the ladder of earthly success, I will be a success in Your eyes if I maintain a good work ethic. I don't want to be someone who is always looking for the next get-rich-quick scheme. Bless me, Lord, with discernment and skill so I can please You in my work all the days of my life. In Jesus' name, I pray. Amen.

Peace in My Work

*People who work hard sleep well, whether
they eat little or much. But the rich
seldom get a good night's sleep.*

ECCLESIASTES 5:12 NLT

Thank You, heavenly Father, that I can lay my head on my pillow at night and rest. There is great peace to be found in knowing that I am working hard to help provide for my family. I am not interested in being rich. Wealth sometimes brings more trouble than it's worth! I just want to continue to honor You in my work and to be content. Thank You for the serenity that is found in simply putting in a good day's work. Giving it my all. Staying the course. Sticking to it when the going gets tough. Holding my tongue and keeping my cool. Accomplishing the tasks set before me day by day. I love You and I thank You. I know that every good and perfect gift comes down from the Father of Lights. I know that my job is a gift from You, and I pray I will always remember to treat it as such. I ask that You would help me to rest easy in the knowledge that I am working hard and honoring my God. It is in Jesus' name, I pray. Amen.

God, Grant Me Serenity
In My Church

Peace in My Church

*"Now I say to you that you are Peter (which means 'rock'),
and upon this rock I will build my church, and all the
powers of hell will not conquer it."*

MATTHEW 16:18 NLT

God, Your Church has always been important to You, from the very start. You are our Great Shepherd; and when we gather together to worship You, You find it pleasing. I ask You, Father, to grant me serenity in my church. The members of this wonderful community bless me in so many ways. There are times, though, when I grow frustrated. We are one body but made up of many types. We all have unique personalities and gifts. We come into conflict at times and disagree over little things—styles of worship, how things should be done, or who should do what. None of it really matters in the long run, Father. What matters is that we are in one accord, seeking to show the world who Christ is and how He has altered our lives. Help my church to be a place of peace. Help me not to sit back and hope things will improve, but help me to truly seek to be part of the solution. Where there is strife, help me to be a peacemaker. I thank You for my church, my pastor, our leaders, and the whole congregation. Each member is a blessing and is so special to You. Help us to see one another as You see us, Lord. Help us to value each other's opinions and ways. These things I ask humbly in the powerful name of Jesus. Amen.

Praying Protection over My Church

But Saul was going everywhere to destroy the church.
He went from house to house, dragging out both
men and women to throw them into prison.

ACTS 8:3 NLT

Heavenly Father, I ask for Your protection over Your Church. Just as Saul, before his conversion, was seeking to destroy the Church, so many outside forces seek to harm Christians today. We come together to worship and to learn more about You, yet there is darkness at every turn. Satan would love nothing more than to enter into Your most holy place and corrupt it with his evil. He is a sneaky one. In the little things, he causes us to argue and judge one another. Help us to resist such temptations. Bring about in Your Church, Lord, a great realization of the times in which we live. Guide us to see that we must bond together and not be torn apart. Nothing will destroy Your Church. You declare that there will always be a remnant of Your people. Let my church be one that pleases You in all we do, and help us to live and worship and serve in harmony with one another. In Jesus' name, I pray. Amen.

A Praying Church

But while Peter was in prison,
the church prayed very earnestly for him.

ACTS 12:5 NLT

Help us, God, to be a praying church. It is easy in this day and age to think we can do things by our own strength. We have so much technology at our fingertips to make lights and music glorious. We have resources and money to do things within the walls of our church. We start planning classes and events and conferences; and sometimes, in the midst of all the good, we forget the best. You are all that matters. You are the Alpha and the Omega. The Beginning and the End. You are sovereign over all things. If we do not emphasize prayer in our church, we are missing the mark entirely. Help us to stop working long enough to pray. All the programs in the world do not begin to compare to prayer. I pray that my church will find great peace in knowing that we are bathing every decision in prayer. Then we will know that we are on the right track and pleasing You, God. Help us to pray for one another even as the church lifted Peter up to You while he was imprisoned. Remind us to pray earnestly for the body of Christ. It is in Jesus' name, I pray. Amen.

Church Growth

*So the churches were strengthened in their
faith and grew larger every day.*

ACTS 16:5 NLT

God, thank You for my church. I love the people who gather there together in Your name. We have become a family—the body of Christ in this community. There are people whom I can count on, and people who can count on me. It feels good to belong, to be a part of something bigger than myself. Help us, Father, to grow—both in our faith and in numbers. It isn't the numbers themselves that we seek but the souls that we know need to be saved by Jesus. May we never grow so comfortable in who we are as a body that we neglect reaching out beyond our walls. I want my church to be a place where people can come and feel welcomed. It should feel like a welcoming family, ready to include all who enter in. Bring growth to our church, Lord, and help me to be a part of that growth. In Jesus' name, I pray. Amen.

One Spirit

*So then, let us aim for harmony in the church
and try to build each other up.*

ROMANS 14:19 NLT

Heavenly Father, I love the word *harmony*. Please bless my church always with peace and tranquility. The world seeks to tear us down, but Your Church is a place where we can build one another up instead. Give us Your eyes to see one another as precious and cherished. When we form committees or start planning and deciding, give us one spirit. There is an old song that says, "They will know we are Christians by our love." May we always be a church that is known for our love, Lord. Bless us with a deep, abiding love for You as our sovereign Lord and for one another in the body of Christ. Help us to love the foreigner and the stranger well. Help us to be a place of peace for those who are hurting. Help us to be a refuge for the weary. Your Church is, in a sense, a hospital. May we minister to those who are wounded and encourage them in the faith. It is in Jesus' name, I ask for harmony in my church. Amen.

Unity in God's Church

First, I hear that there are divisions among you when you meet as a church, and to some extent I believe it.

1 CORINTHIANS 11:18 NLT

Heavenly Father, may there be no divisions within my church. It isn't my church, after all. It isn't the pastor's church. It doesn't belong to us. It belongs to You. It is Your Church. Your Church should not look like the world with all of its strife and conflict. It should stand out as different. It should be a haven for people, not a place of hostility. May we come together as one body with one spirit. May we seek unity in the Lord Jesus above all else. Help us to major on the majors and not the minors. Help us to resist the urge to make mountains out of molehills. In times when we feel wronged, help us to come together and converse rather than assuming the worst about our brothers and sisters. Such amazing grace You have poured out on each of us! May we, in turn, show grace to each other. I know that we will experience great peace within our church when we choose unity over division. In Jesus' name, I pray. Amen.

Truth in Love

Instead, we will speak the truth in love,
growing in every way more and more like
Christ, who is the head of his body, the church.

EPHESIANS 4:15 NLT

Heavenly Father, to speak the truth in love is not always easy. Sometimes there are disagreements within my church. Other times there are believers who stray and need correction. Help my church and its leaders know how to speak the truth in love. Each situation is so unique, but help us to remember that they all involve people. And people are Your most precious creation, Your masterpieces that bear Your signature and image. Help us to value human life and to remember that it is often more fragile than it seems. There are times when correction must happen, but let it be done in love and with Your Spirit. Help us to love all people and to realize that we too go astray. We are all sinners and lose sight of the right ways at times. I ask that we will be led always to speak the truth in love within my church. In this way we will grow more and more like Jesus, which is always our goal. In His name, I pray. Amen.

God, Grant Me Serenity
IN MY THOUGHTS

Your Will for My Life

Give me understanding and I will obey your instructions;
I will put them into practice with all my heart.

PSALM 119:34 NLT

God, fill my thoughts with understanding. I know that when I am able to comprehend Your will for my life, I will follow gladly in Your ways. I want to please You with all of my thoughts. I make a lot of plans for my own life, but I pray that I will always be attentive to the signs and factors that You use to direct me. I know that true peace and serenity will only be mine when I am led by Your hand. I want Your will for my life more than I want to go my own way. Father, give me an obedient heart. I will seek Your ways and listen to Your instructions. I will read Your Word in order to discover the truths You want me to live by. Help me to put Your ways into practice with all of my heart. In Jesus' name, I pray. Amen.

Think on Noble Things

*Finally, brothers and sisters, whatever is true, whatever is noble,
whatever is right, whatever is pure, whatever is lovely,
whatever is admirable—if anything is excellent
or praiseworthy—think about such things.*

PHILIPPIANS 4:8 NIV

Heavenly Father, may my thought life be pure, and may it honor You, my God. So many times my thoughts drift to selfish pursuits. I think about what I want or need. I dwell on what I don't have rather than focusing on all of Your many blessings. I think negative thoughts about those around me, when, in reality, I should know that we are all struggling. No one is perfect. I focus at times on how someone has hurt me when I should pray for that individual instead. I read in Your Word that You desire for me to think on noble things. Right things. That which is pure. That which is lovely, admirable, excellent, and praiseworthy. As I still my heart and mind before You, I ask that You would bring such things to my mind. Help me to focus on praising You. You are great and greatly to be praised. Bring to mind all that I have been blessed with so that I will be filled with a grateful heart. May I dwell on Your Word, which is truth, and Your character, which is altogether lovely. May I think on things with substance and consequence—kingdom matters. In Jesus' name, I ask You to make my thoughts pleasing unto You, Father. Amen.

Renew My Mind

Do not conform to the pattern of this world,
but be transformed by the renewing of your mind.
Then you will be able to test and approve what
God's will is—his good, pleasing and perfect will.

ROMANS 12:2 NIV

Renew my mind, heavenly Father, so that my thoughts might please You and my actions reflect Your great love. As a believer in Christ Jesus, just as believers who have gone before me, I must not conform to the ways of this world. The world calls out to do whatever feels good, to live in the moment, to think only about myself and what makes me happy. The world offers experiences through drugs and alcohol, through things that money can buy, and through keeping up—always striving to keep up—with the Joneses. The world does not value You or Your ways, which are holy and righteous. Show me a different way, O Lord. Illuminate the path before me and shine Your light into the recesses of my mind. In those times when I am tempted to go the way of the world, draw me back, I pray. Train my mind and my heart to long for You and You alone. In Jesus' name, I pray. Amen.

Truth, Like Treasure

My child, never forget the things I have taught you.
Store my commands in your heart. If you do this, you will
live many years, and your life will be satisfying. Never let
loyalty and kindness leave you! Tie them around your neck
as a reminder. Write them deep within your heart.

PROVERBS 3:1–3 NLT

God, like precious jewels stored in a treasure chest, I will store Your teachings in my heart of hearts. May I always have Your commands in my thoughts, and may I honor You in all that I do as a result. May loyalty and kindness be like a bull's-eye target that I wake up each day aiming to hit. Certainly, at times, I will miss the mark, but I want to seek to be like Jesus in all of my interactions. In the deepest parts of my soul, may I keep reminders of Your great love and all of Your ways. You are my Father, and I, created in Your perfect image, want to love as You love and be faithful as You are faithful. You tell me that true satisfaction comes from remembering what You have taught me and living out Your will on this earth. Hold me close, Father, and whisper Your truth and Your love over me. In Jesus' name, I pray. Amen.

Direct My Paths

*Trust in the LORD with all your heart; do not depend on
your own understanding. Seek his will in all you do,
and he will show you which path to take.*

PROVERBS 3:5–6 NLT

Heavenly Father, I trust You. Help me to trust You even more. I
want to trust in You so fully that when I come to a fork in the road
and have a decision to make, I instantly—on impulse—look to
You. I am just a mere human, a woman. I don't have the wisdom
to know even a fraction of what You know. You see my life as a
beautiful tapestry. You see all the threads and colors woven together
to create a wondrous picture. You see the beginning and the end.
You see everything in between. I see one little section at a time. I
need You to help me understand and follow hard after You. This
world calls out to me with many voices. It seems that everywhere
I turn, I have to fight temptations to walk on paths I know lead
to nowhere. I want to walk on paths of righteousness. I want to
honor You, my God. In Jesus' name, I ask for wisdom. Amen.

Think on Heavenly Things

*Think about the things of heaven, not the things of earth. For you
died to this life, and your real life is hidden with Christ in God. And
when Christ, who is your life, is revealed to the whole world, you
will share in all his glory. So put to death the sinful, earthly things
lurking within you. Have nothing to do with sexual immorality,
impurity, lust, and evil desires. Don't be greedy, for a greedy person
is an idolater, worshiping the things of this world.*

COLOSSIANS 3:2–5 NLT

Heavenly Father, I know that this earth is not my home. I am but
a visitor here, an alien, one who is passing through but who does
not truly belong. My identity is in You. My old life has gone, and
my new life is hidden with my Jesus in You. Help me, I pray, to
put any sinful ways to rest. Cast away from my mind every sinful
thought. I don't want death lurking where there should only be
life. I don't desire the things of this world. But I do desire Your
ways, Father, which are always higher and always best for Your
children. Remove from my heart any fragment of greed or remnant
of a past life of sin. I refuse to be a prisoner, even in my thoughts.
I am free in Christ, and I will no longer worship the empty things
of this world. I want my life to be a vessel of worship for You, my
King. In Jesus' name, I pray. Amen.

Focus on God

Let your eyes look straight ahead;
fix your gaze directly before you.

PROVERBS 4:25 NIV

Heavenly Father, please help me fix my gaze on You. I know that whatever I am focused on is where I will end up. If I focus on the world, the world will consume me. If I set You before me as my target, my goal, and my destination, You will be where I end up! I want to honor You and live for You. I find the greatest peace in times when I know I am right in the midst of Your will, Father. You tell me in Your Word not to look to the right or to the left but to look straight ahead. When I look around, I see so many things to worry about or to lead me off the right path. But when I look directly at You, I see nothing but Your glory. I am filled with a sense of calm. I am secure in my Father's care. I know that You are my guide and my provider. Just as little sheep depend upon the sound of their shepherd's voice, I depend upon You to direct me. Keep me always focused on You. In Jesus' name, I pray. Amen.

Thinking of Others

Don't be selfish; don't try to impress others. Be humble, thinking of others as better than yourselves. Don't look out only for your own interests, but take an interest in others, too.

PHILIPPIANS 2:3–4 NLT

God, please keep me from selfish thinking. Help me to think of others before myself, never as less than or not as important. In my humanity, I look out for number one. But I am not a slave to my humanity any longer. I have Christ in my heart. I am a new creation. I can, in His power, look beyond myself and my desires and even my needs. I can think of those around me. I can see their struggles. I can feel their pain. I can think of how my words and actions will impact them. I can be proactive in caring for those within my church community and my workplace. I can move beyond the natural to the supernatural. I can be "Jesus with skin on" to those in need. I may be the only Jesus some will ever see. Jesus was a servant leader on this earth. May I follow in His footsteps. May I think of others first. In Christ's name, I pray. Amen.

Take Every Thought Captive

*We demolish arguments and every pretension that sets itself up
against the knowledge of God, and we take captive
every thought to make it obedient to Christ.*

2 Corinthians 10:5 niv

God, I will choose today to take every thought captive to my Jesus. I know that as my thought life goes, so goes my spiritual life. Please don't let my thoughts lead me to unholy places. Keep me from conflict and arguments. Keep me from sin, I pray. As soon as a thought begins to creep into my mind that may not be a righteous thought, may I recognize it and take it captive to Christ. May Christ be the center of my existence. May my responses and my reactions bear His image. May I be known by friends and family members as one who follows Jesus and not one who just gives Christianity lip service. May my heart and my mind and my very soul be so like that of Jesus that others will see my Savior in me. Clear my mind now as I come before You in prayer and in surrender. My mind is a battleground. Every day that I live in this fallen world, Satan will try to sway me into negative and defeated thinking. But with the power of the cross of Jesus, I will resist his empty temptations to think in such a way. Help me to truly surrender my thoughts to You. In Jesus' name, I ask these things. Amen.

God, Grant Me Serenity
IN MY EMOTIONS

Anxious for Nothing

Do not be anxious about anything, but in every situation,
by prayer and petition, with thanksgiving, present your requests
to God. And the peace of God, which transcends all understanding,
will guard your hearts and your minds in Christ Jesus.

PHILIPPIANS 4:6–7 NIV

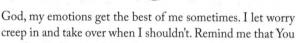

God, my emotions get the best of me sometimes. I let worry creep in and take over when I shouldn't. Remind me that You are always there, and You hear my prayers. Please help me not to let my emotions take control, but give me the presence of mind to take every thought captive to Christ. When I am under stress, I will take in a deep breath and let it out slowly. I will exhale, knowing that You have me in the palm of Your hand. You are bigger and greater than any fear or concern life may bring. You are my peace giver, my delight, my rest. I claim the power of Christ over my emotions, and I gladly surrender all of my anxiety at the foot of Your throne. Please comfort me through the Holy Spirit, and remind me of Your constant care. In Jesus' name, I pray. Amen.

Not Letting Emotions Rule over Me

A happy heart makes the face cheerful,
but heartache crushes the spirit.

PROVERBS 15:13 NIV

God, please replace any negativity in me with a smile. I have heard it said that attitude is a little thing that makes a big difference, and I believe that to be true. When I allow circumstances to dictate my emotions, I quickly go down a road that leads to depression and sadness. But when I, instead, choose to look on the bright side, my heart is lifted and my whole self follows. Bring a peace that passes all understanding to my heart, I pray. A peace that this world cannot offer. A peace that is available only to the believer, only to the one whose trust is in You. I know that every day won't be easy in this life. This is a fallen world, and due to sin there are going to be really hard times. But I pray that I will learn to count even the trials as joy, knowing that trials develop character in me and make me more like Jesus. It is in His name, I pray this prayer. Amen.

Jesus Wept

When Jesus saw her weeping, and the Jews who had come along with her also weeping, he was deeply moved in spirit and troubled. "Where have you laid him?" he asked. "Come and see, Lord," they replied. Jesus wept.

JOHN 11:33–35 NIV

Jesus, You wept. You were moved by the grief of others and by the death of Your beloved friend. You experienced real emotion. You were human, and yet God. You chose this place in all of its sin; You chose earth—for me. You left heaven, where there are no tears, to come dwell here with us. You walked in our shoes. You hurt like we hurt. Thank You for that. Thank You for crying so I know You understand when I cry. Thank You for catching my tears and for comforting me, Father. You are good. You are *always* good. And You love me with a depth that could bring You to tears—just as You wept over the loss of Lazarus. I am so blessed to be loved like that. Thank You for coming to earth and experiencing painful emotions so that I might know You understand the things I feel. I love You, Lord. In Your powerful name, I pray. Amen.

Resisting Sin as a Result of Anger

*"In your anger do not sin": Do not let the sun go down while
you are still angry, and do not give the devil a foothold.*

EPHESIANS 4:26–27 NIV

I get angry, Lord. I know I can't hide it from You. You have seen
it and heard it. You know all about my emotions—even the ones
that aren't so sweet. The lesson You have for me in Ephesians is
not that I would never get angry; it's that I wouldn't sin as a result
of my anger. Tame my anger, Lord. Help me to snuff it out while
it's just a spark, before it catches hold and becomes a wild and
raging fire. Give me the grace with others to hold my tongue and
take a deep breath. Give me patience so that I might not blow
up in a rage over something that really doesn't warrant such a
strong reaction. I don't want Satan to have any power in my life.
I want to walk with You and in Your ways all the days of my life.
May I never sin in anger, Father. And on those days when anger
does creep in, help me to apologize and make things right before
I go to bed at night. I love You, Lord, and I want to please You. I
know that You have the power to diffuse my anger before it gets
out of control. Please set a guard over my heart and mind, that
anger would not be a problem in my life. In Jesus' name, amen.

The Comfort of the Holy Spirit

"Blessed are those who mourn,
for they will be comforted."

MATTHEW 5:4 NIV

Lord, I am an emotional creature. I was created to experience emotions. I feel deeply. I rejoice and laugh. I also hurt and cry. It's just part of being human. It's who I am. At times, I mourn. I weep in deep grief over someone or something lost. I experience grief when I lose a loved one. I feel it when I lose a long-held dream. When something that means so much is taken from me, it is natural that I would grieve. Comfort me in such times, Lord. May I sense the presence of the Holy Spirit, the One You sent to be with me while we are apart. You have told me You have gone to heaven to prepare a place for me so that I might spend eternity with You. You have left the Holy Spirit in Your place, and one of His main jobs is to serve as the Comforter. This brings me a lot of peace, knowing that You predicted I would need such help. When You ascended into heaven, You thought of me. You saw into my future. You saw the grief, and You didn't want me to cry alone. You wanted me to have a Comforter. Thank You for that, Jesus. Thank You for the sweet comfort of Your Holy Spirit that I sense near me even now. In Your name, I pray. Amen.

Seek Peace and Pursue It

Turn from evil and do good; seek peace and pursue it.

PSALM 34:14 NIV

Heavenly Father, my emotions can lead me astray—and quickly! When I am sad or angry, I can easily go down the wrong road. I start condemning myself or others, creating burdens that we are not meant to bear. I say things I don't mean. I act in a manner that does not reflect the Gospel of Christ. Help me in these moments to stop and simply turn to You. Help me turn from evil and instead choose what is good and right. Help me to seek peace and to chase after it. Help me to lead a peaceful life no matter the cost. If I lose a friendship because someone is just too conflict-prone over an extended period of time, then teach me to cut my losses. There may be a price to pay for peace sometimes. I pray that I would be a pursuer of peace and serenity and that I would not dishonor You because of emotions that have run wild and taken me off course. In Jesus' name, I pray for control over my emotions. I pray for peace. Amen.

It Is Well with My Soul

Dear friend, I pray that you may enjoy good health and that all may go well with you, even as your soul is getting along well.

3 JOHN 1:2 NIV

Father God, it is well with my soul. My body and mind are connected. They really can't be considered separately, because one affects the other so greatly. Thank You that I have found the secret to being at peace on the inside, regardless of my outward circumstances. The apostle Paul wrote that he had learned to be content in any circumstances, and I pray the same is true in my life. I hope that no matter what happens, I will maintain a wellness in my soul—a peace that is deep and abiding—because I know I am Yours. I know You are my God. I know that no matter what happens in this life, I have the hope of heaven. I would love to enjoy good health physically all the days of my life, but I long even more for an inward peace and serenity even into my old age. Thank You, Lord, that with Jesus in my heart I can truly say it is well with my soul. In His name, I pray. Amen.

Self-Control

*God did not give us a spirit that makes us afraid
but a spirit of power and love and self-control.*

2 TIMOTHY 1:7 NCV

Dear God, thank You for promising me that I don't have to fear.
I have been given a spirit of power, love, and self-control. I have
power over my emotions in the name of Jesus. I can control how I
react when I am tapped into Your power source. I find that if I'm
not spending time in the Word and in prayer, I am less likely to
respond calmly when I'm hit with a stressful situation. Thank You
that You have put Your power in me. The same power that raised
Jesus from the dead lives inside of me; and through that power,
I am more than a conqueror. I am able to control my emotions
instead of my emotions controlling me. Thank You, Lord, for
self-control. What a gift! Tame my tongue, Father. Help me to
keep a lid on my anger. Teach me to breathe. Teach me to count
to ten or step away before I react emotionally in the heat of the
moment. I have what it takes to exercise self-discipline, so please
help me to make it a reality in my life. I won't always react per-
fectly, but I can learn to be a woman who controls her emotions.
In Jesus' name, I pray. Amen.

God, Grant Me Serenity
IN MY STRENGTHS AND WEAKNESSES

In Christ's Strength

I can do all things through him who strengthens me.

PHILIPPIANS 4:13 ESV

God, I may be better at some things than others. We all are. I have my strengths and weaknesses just like the next woman. But the Bible tells me that I can do all things through Christ, who strengthens me. *All things.* I think this means that anything I am called to do, I will have the strength to accomplish. If I am called to be a single woman, I can do it through Christ, who strengthens me. If I am called to be married, I can be a wife to my husband in Christ's strength. If You give me children, I can parent with the strength given to me by my Jesus. If I face hardships, I can walk through them because Jesus walks with me. He will guide me, assist me, and at times completely carry me through life. There is nothing that I cannot do because I have the power of Jesus Christ alive and well within my soul. On my own, I can do nothing. With Jesus, it is quite the opposite. He is a game changer. He makes the ending of my story so much more magnificent than the beginning. I can do *all things* through my Jesus. It is in His name, I pray. Amen.

In His Image

So God created man in his own image, in the image of God he created him; male and female he created them.

GENESIS 1:27 ESV

Father God, I am created in Your image. You made everything in the world, but Your final masterpiece was mankind. You were not satisfied with Your created world until you placed man and woman in the garden. I am their descendant. I bear Your image, just as they did. When I look in the mirror, I see my weaknesses. They go far deeper than my outward appearance. I realize I am so very limited. I recognize that there are many things I don't do well. I fail You every day, Father. I know it is part of being human, but I still beat myself up for it. I want to be perfect. I want to do things well and to be smart and attractive and. . .enough. I admit I struggle with wanting to be *enough*. But I hear You whisper to me, *"Daughter, you are enough."* It is by grace I am saved. Thank You, Father, for making me in Your image and saving me through Your Son. I am humbly aware that I have many weaknesses, but I thank You that I am seen as enough by my Father. You see me through a Jesus lens, and I am Your precious daughter. What a blessing, God. In Jesus' name, I pray. Amen.

Power in Weakness

*He gives strength to those who are tired
and more power to those who are weak.*

ISAIAH 40:29 NCV

God of all power, thank You for being my power source. When I am weak, You are strong. Just as the children's song says: "Jesus loves me. This I know—for the Bible tells me so. Little ones to Him belong. I am weak, but He is strong. Yes, Jesus loves me!" What a blessing to know that I am not expected to or required to be the best at everything. There will always be areas of my life in which I am weak. I may be good at hospitality but not gifted in teaching children's Sunday school. I may be a wonderful behind-the-scenes helper, but being in charge of a ministry may scare me to death! I am not created with all of the spiritual gifts, but the ones I have I am responsible for using for Your kingdom. And when I am called upon to do something that takes me way out of my comfort zone, I need not fear. You are with me, and You will forever be my power source. I can tap into the power available to me through Christ anytime and in any place. I surrender my weaknesses to You, Lord, for in You I am strong. In Jesus' name, I pray. Amen.

One Body, Many Parts

Together you are the body of Christ,
and each one of you is a part of that body.

1 CORINTHIANS 12:27 NCV

God, help me to remember that while I am not good at everything, I have been given gifts. And I am to use them for Your glory. The body of Christ is an amazing thing. I look around and see those who are so very different from me. It's difficult not to be envious of others' talents and abilities. Many have been gifted with a beautiful singing voice or the gift of mercy, while those are not my specialities! But I need to remember that You are the one who chose how I should be gifted. I will focus today on my strengths, not my weaknesses. I will find ways to use my talents to bring honor to Your name. I am part of the body, and I play an important role that no one else can play. There is a contemporary Christian song that says it this way, and I dwell upon these words today as I pray: "You are made to fill a purpose that only you could do, so there could never be a more beautiful you!" In Jesus' name, I ask that I would be aware of my gifts and that I will always use them for Your kingdom, Lord. Amen.

Different Gifts

*There are different kinds of gifts, but they are all from the same
Spirit. There are different ways to serve but the same Lord to serve.
And there are different ways that God works through people but the
same God. God works in all of us in everything we do. Something
from the Spirit can be seen in each person, for the common good.*

1 CORINTHIANS 12:4–7 NCV

God, I love the way the Holy Spirit works. We are all gifted, yet
in so many different ways. May my gifts be seen, and may they
be used for the common good of Your people. Just as a mother or
father may not give each child the exact same clothing item but
rather what is needed at the time, the Holy Spirit knows what
we need. If a child needs a new pair of shoes, his mother does
not buy him a coat. If another has outgrown her coat, she is not
given a new pair of shoes. In the wisdom and sovereignty of the
Holy Ghost, it was determined that I would receive the gifts I
have received. May I never question You or grumble about what
I wish I could do instead. I want to live my life in service to You,
God, and as a servant for Your people. May everything I do reflect
this type of attitude. Thank You for the gifts You have blessed
me with, and help me to recognize the responsibility that comes
with my strengths and abilities. In Jesus' name, I pray. Amen.

Bearing Fruit

*"I am the vine, and you are the branches. If any remain in
me and I remain in them, they produce much fruit.
But without me they can do nothing."*

JOHN 15:5 NCV

Heavenly Father, I want to bear fruit for Your kingdom. I don't want to try to do things in my own strength any longer. I have talents and abilities, but when I become proud—thinking how good I am and how much I can do for You—I am instantly taken down a notch. There is nothing in and of myself that is pleasing to You, Lord. I need You every moment of every hour in order to bear fruit. And so I must abide in You. Keep me close to Your side, Father. Never let me stray. As I spend time in Your scriptures, dwelling upon and meditating on Your words, I abide in You. As I sit still and pray, giving You time to speak to me, I abide in You. And as I abide in You, I will bear more and more fruit for Your kingdom. I do not wish to do it on my own, as I am incapable. Without You, I can do nothing; but through the power of Your Spirit, I am able to shine for the kingdom. In Jesus' name, I ask that I would always abide in You and that I would bear much fruit. Someday, I want to hear these words: *"Well done, good and faithful servant. Well done."* Amen.

Work vs. Rest

*"Come to me, all of you who are tired and have heavy loads,
and I will give you rest. Accept my teachings and learn
from me, because I am gentle and humble in spirit,
and you will find rest for your lives."*

MATTHEW 11:28–29 NCV

Sometimes, Father, I grow weary. I work and strive and try to accomplish so much. I use my gifts. I serve. I join the choir or a committee. I go on a mission trip. I hone my gifts, and then I use them for Your glory. But, in doing so, I often wear myself out. I know exhaustion isn't Your plan for me. Help me to strike the right balance between serving and resting, between using my gifts and simply finding solace in Your presence. Just as Mary and Martha, the two sisters, struggled over what was best—sitting at Your feet or working to serve You—I find the same question relevant in my own life. Should I be a Mary or a Martha? At times I try to do too much. Calm my spirit. Show me when to work and when to rest. Remind me that You are here to bear my heavy load and that when it all just gets to be too much, I am free to say no to some things. I am free to rest in Your presence. Oh how I need that, Lord. In Jesus' name, I pray. Amen.

Resisting Pride in My Strengths

*Don't praise yourself. Let someone else do it. Let the praise
come from a stranger and not from your own mouth.*

PROVERBS 27:2 NCV

Heavenly Father, sometimes I am proud of the things I do well.
It's like there's a motor inside, propelling me to do better than
others. While I know it's good to be motivated and driven,
please keep me from growing prideful. The gifts and abilities I
have been blessed with are for Your glory, not mine. Allow me
to use my gifts well and to learn and grow—not for self-glory,
but in honor of my King. I have heard it said that "pride goeth
before a fall." I understand that praise should come from others
and not from myself. I should be at work for an audience of
one—You, my heavenly Father. I love You, Lord, and I thank You
for the strengths You have bestowed upon me. Whatever I do,
let me do it to the best of my ability—and not for the praise
of men but in order to bring glory to You. In Jesus' name, I
pray. Amen.

God, Grant Me Serenity
IN MY UNCERTAINTY

Focus on the Present

"Give your entire attention to what God is doing right now, and don't get worked up about what may or may not happen tomorrow. God will help you deal with whatever hard things come up when the time comes."

MATTHEW 6:34 MSG

Heavenly Father, I worry too much. You've told me not to worry about tomorrow but to focus on what You are doing today—in this hour, in this very moment. I could dwell on all the what-ifs of life, or I can choose to lay them down at Your feet. There is no use in pondering all the possibilities. This kind of thinking leads to gloom and doom. I don't want to live with a sense of dread but with a lightness in my step. I am a believer in Jesus; He has made me new. My old life has gone, and my new life should reflect an inner trust and peace in knowing Him. Father God, hard things will come. This is a fallen world in which we live, and I am promised that there will be trials and tribulations. But You will see me through those troubles one step at a time. Remind me to enjoy the moment, God. Remind me to savor the serenity of walking through life with a Savior who will never leave or forsake me. There is great peace in trusting Jesus with my future. In His name, I pray. Amen.

God Protects Me

The LORD will protect you from all dangers;
he will guard your life. The LORD will guard you
as you come and go, both now and forever.

PSALM 121:7–8 NCV

Lord, I am unsure about the future. There are so many question marks where there used to be periods! Everything seemed clear and so secure, but now the unknown has invaded and I am at a standstill, not knowing what to do. I need Your reassurance that You are with me. You guard me and protect me because I am Yours. Everything may seem up in the air, but You have not lost sight of me. You keep watch over all my comings and goings. Throughout the day and into the night, You sing over me, Father. You comfort me with Your presence. I am never alone. Even in the face of an unknown future, I will place my trust in You. You have never let me down before, and You aren't about to start! Thank You, Father, for Your steadfast love. Thank You for the promise that You will never let me go. In the name of Your Son, Jesus, I pray. Amen.

Don't Worry

"Don't worry and say, 'What will we eat?' or 'What will we drink?' or 'What will we wear?' The people who don't know God keep trying to get these things, and your Father in heaven knows you need them. Seek first God's kingdom and what God wants. Then all your other needs will be met as well. So don't worry about tomorrow, because tomorrow will have its own worries. Each day has enough trouble of its own."

MATTHEW 6:31–34 NCV

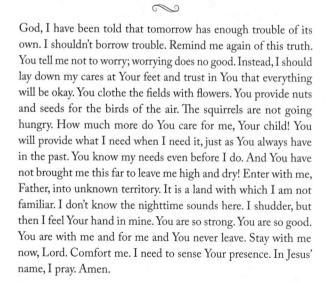

God, I have been told that tomorrow has enough trouble of its own. I shouldn't borrow trouble. Remind me again of this truth. You tell me not to worry; worrying does no good. Instead, I should lay down my cares at Your feet and trust in You that everything will be okay. You clothe the fields with flowers. You provide nuts and seeds for the birds of the air. The squirrels are not going hungry. How much more do You care for me, Your child! You will provide what I need when I need it, just as You always have in the past. You know my needs even before I do. And You have not brought me this far to leave me high and dry! Enter with me, Father, into unknown territory. It is a land with which I am not familiar. I don't know the nighttime sounds here. I shudder, but then I feel Your hand in mine. You are so strong. You are so good. You are with me and for me and You never leave. Stay with me now, Lord. Comfort me. I need to sense Your presence. In Jesus' name, I pray. Amen.

The Plans God Has for Me

"For I know the plans I have for you," declares the LORD,
"plans to prosper you and not to harm you,
plans to give you hope and a future."

JEREMIAH 29:11 NIV

Lord, You know the plans You have for me. You see the future even though it is so unclear to me. I stand here very uncertain of what tomorrow holds, but You are never uncertain. You know the number of hairs on my head. You know my strengths and weaknesses. You knit me together in my mother's womb. All of the days You have planned for my life are written in Your book. You are my Creator and my Sustainer. You are the Great I Am. You are what I need in every moment. You are my King of Glory and my Prince of Peace. You are the Bread of Life that sustains me. You are manna from heaven, day by day. You meet my needs and show me just a few steps ahead at a time. You do not reveal to me more than I can handle. You shine Your light on my next step, and I take it in faith that You will direct me when it is time to step out again. I find great serenity in knowing You go before me—that You know the plans—because You are the One who made them. I love You, Lord. In Jesus' name, I pray. Amen.

God Is with Me

"The LORD your God is with you, the Mighty Warrior who saves.
He will take great delight in you; in his love he will no longer
rebuke you, but will rejoice over you with singing."

ZEPHANIAH 3:17 NIV

Heavenly Father, I find peace when I read in Zephaniah that You will rejoice over me with singing. The Lord my God is with me. That is such a wonderful promise! So many religions are empty. People worship statues that have no life and that offer no life to them in return. They follow a multitude of lowercase *g* gods, completely unaware of the one true God. You are sovereign over all things. You created the world and breathed man into existence. You are the Mighty Warrior who saves us from Satan, who would love to steal and kill and destroy his way into our lives. Believers in Christ have nothing to fear because You are always fighting for us. There are battles I cannot see in the spiritual realms. You defend Your own against the evil one. As I feel myself beginning to fear the future and all of life's uncertainty, I fix my eyes again on Jesus. I see Him there on the cross, dying for my sin. That kind of love is beautifully unfathomable. It is not found in golden calves. It is not offered by Allah or Muhammad. It is not available in the Buddhist temple or in the mosque. It comes only from the one true God. I reach out to You now, in faith, in the face of a very uncertain future. And I cling to my very certain God. In Jesus' name, I pray. Amen.

God Has Great Plans for Me

However, as it is written: "What no eye has seen, what no ear has heard, and what no human mind has conceived"—the things God has prepared for those who love him.

1 CORINTHIANS 2:9 NIV

Father God, I cannot see what lies ahead, but why do I assume so often that it's something bad? Your Word refreshes me today. It promises me that no eye has seen, no ear has heard, no human mind has conceived the things You have prepared for those who love You. Wow! I think of Christmas as a child. I would lie awake and try to imagine what Santa would bring for me and place under the tree. I couldn't even begin to imagine! And how much greater are the wonderful things You have planned for me, Eternal God. When I look at Your universe, I see Your handiwork. I see it on display in the magnificent sunsets and the glorious sunrises. You paint rainbows in the sky. You have dotted the earth with rushing waterfalls and creatively designed animals of all kinds. You have a wild imagination, Father! To think that You have such wonderful and wild plans for me! I can rest easy, remembering that the future—my future—is in Your capable hands. In Jesus' name, I pray. Amen.

God, Grant Me Serenity
IN MY MARRIAGE OR SINGLENESS

Love Deeply

Above all, love each other deeply,
because love covers over a multitude of sins.

1 PETER 4:8 NIV

God, I read in Your Word that You are love. I personally have experienced Your eternal love, Your amazing grace. And yet I struggle, at times, to love my husband. It was all so easy in the beginning. The white dress was fun to select, and the wedding was beautiful. Now the reality of day by day, month by month, year by year has set in. It's not all quite as glamorous as it looks in the photos in the big white photo album on our coffee table. Love is hard. It requires a lot of me. But when I love my husband well, it feels so good. When I look past his little faults and remember the blessing of the man You have put in my life to be my husband. . . When I forgive. . . When I serve him and meet his needs. . . When I see him as You see him—faultless, blameless, righteous, forgiven, and free. . .because he is Your child, saved by the same grace that You have poured out on me. Help me to love my husband deeply, for love covers a multitude of sins. He is not perfect; nor am I! But I will love him well. And in doing so, I will love You, Lord. In Jesus' name, I ask You to help me to love deeply beyond the fairy tale and into the trenches of marriage. Amen.

Becoming One

"And the two will become one flesh.'
So they are no longer two, but one flesh."

MARK 10:8 NIV

Marriage is a mystery, God—a mystery of two becoming one. I sometimes feel the strongest bond with my husband. I understand that we are one now. However, I often feel very, very separate from him. He doesn't always understand me. He doesn't pay attention to the details that I would like him to notice. He acts in ways that frustrate me. Remind me, Lord, in such moments, that this man is not a separate entity but part of me now. He is my husband, for better or for worse, all the days of my life. I know that when I honor him, I honor You. And I know that my marriage will be more peaceful when I work at it with all my heart. I must accept his weaknesses and promote his strengths. I must encourage him and respect him, for a man needs to be respected and lifted up by his wife. I must seek to love him even as I love myself—for he is the other part of my heart. Thank You for my husband, Father, and for the unity we share. May our bond always be one that honors You. In Jesus' name, I pray. Amen.

My Husband

*"For this reason a man will leave his father and mother
and be united to his wife, and the two will become one flesh."*

EPHESIANS 5:31 NIV

Heavenly Father, I know that now that I am married, I must truly "leave" my parents. They are so important to me; but sometimes when I rely too heavily on them, it takes away from my marriage. It puts a strain on the relationship between my husband and me. Help me to remember that my husband is number one. I must daily remember what it means to leave and to cleave. I have left my family of origin. While they are still very important to me and I should always honor my parents, I need to draw a line in the sand when it comes to such things as decision-making. My husband takes the lead now. He is my guide. He is the one I will support and find agreement with. Help me to do this with grace. Show me how to honor my mom and dad while still making it clear that my husband is first. In Jesus' name, I ask these things. Amen.

An Excellent Wife

*An excellent wife who can find? She is far more
precious than jewels. The heart of her husband trusts
in her, and he will have no lack of gain. She does
him good, and not harm, all the days of her life.*

PROVERBS 31:10–12 ESV

Heavenly Father, help me to be a wife like the one described in Proverbs 31. I know my home will be a more peaceful place when it's filled with love between my husband and me. We set the tone for our family—our children look to us for an example. One day their marriages will look somewhat like ours because these are the patterns they are seeing. May I love and respect my husband well. I want to be an excellent wife, one who sees a need and meets it without having to be asked. I want to go the extra mile in my marriage. I want to do my husband good and not harm all the days of our lives. Sometimes I am tempted to be selfish. I look to my own needs before I notice his. I must learn to put off self and take on selflessness in order to have a strong marriage. Help me, Lord. In Jesus' name, I pray. Amen.

My Husband's Praise

*Her children rise up and call her blessed; her husband also,
and he praises her: "Many women have done excellently,
but you surpass them all." Charm is deceitful, and beauty is
vain, but a woman who fears the LORD is to be praised.*

PROVERBS 31:28–30 ESV

God, help me not to be dependent upon my husband's praise.
Help me to be a good wife who loves and serves and gives regardless of his reaction. It is wonderful when he notices and praises
me, but ultimately I cannot depend upon it. I must learn to seek
only to honor him and to honor You. You are the one who matters
most. You are my audience of one. You are my God. I hope to
be a wife who makes my husband proud, one whom he is happy
to come home to at the end of the day. I ask You to give me the
wisdom to know when to initiate conversations and when to
remain silent. I ask You to show me my husband's strengths that
I might praise him in those areas. I ask You to reveal to me areas
where he may feel insecure or "not enough" in order that I might
reassure him and build him up. Make me a better wife with each
passing day, I pray, in Jesus' name. Amen.

Love

Love is patient, love is kind. It does not envy, it does not boast,
it is not proud. It does not dishonor others, it is not self-seeking,
it is not easily angered, it keeps no record of wrongs. Love does
not delight in evil but rejoices with the truth. It always protects,
always trusts, always hopes, always perseveres. Love never fails.

1 CORINTHIANS 13:4–8 NIV

Heavenly Father, I want love to look like 1 Corinthians 13 in my household. Help me to love with patience. When my husband frustrates me, help me to hold my tongue. Help me not to be jealous. Truth be told, I sometimes think he has it easier than I do. I am juggling so many roles, and he puts so much into his work. I feel like I have to be Superwoman, and I begin to hold grudges. Tame this emotion in me, Father. I want my heart to be one that honors my husband. Help me not to be self-seeking. When I feel angry, help me to find healthy ways to deal with it. I desire so strongly to resist sinning in my anger. The keeping a record of wrongs is a biggie for me, God. I tend to bring up what he did wrong "last time" every time we argue. Please help me to remove negative words from my vocabulary; they do nothing to improve or strengthen my relationship with my spouse. Help there to be a deep and abiding love present in my marriage—one that protects, trusts, hopes, and perseveres. A love that never fails. In Jesus' name, I pray. Amen.

God Is My Husband

For your Maker is your husband—the LORD Almighty is his name—the Holy One of Israel is your Redeemer; he is called the God of all the earth.

ISAIAH 54:5 NIV

Being single isn't always easy, Lord. You know this. You were single when You walked this earth. You know how I struggle. You see me when I am alone. You hear the weeping at times when it just seems so. . .lonely. It's not an easy road, but neither is marriage. Either way, married or single, we must rely on You. And so, in this season of singleness, be my husband. Comfort me. Listen to me. Hold me close. Remind me of Your deep and abiding love for me. Provide for me, I pray. Please send me constant reminders that I am never alone. You promise me in Your Word that You will never let me go. Thank You for loving me so much. In Jesus' name, I pray. Amen.

God, Grant Me Serenity
IN MOTHERHOOD

A Wise Mother

*My son, keep your father's command and do not forsake
your mother's teaching. Bind them always on
your heart; fasten them around your neck.*

PROVERBS 6:20–21 NIV

Heavenly Father, I ask that You would make me a wise mother. I want to parent my children in a way that honors You at all times. I pray that I would know when and how to discipline my kids. They need instruction, and they need to learn right from wrong. Their father and I are the ones You have appointed for this task, and I pray we will be guided in Your wisdom. I want my home to be one of peace and love. I want my children to grow up learning to be respectful, kind individuals who love and serve You with their lives. I know that I am often not the example I should be and that they learn so much by watching me. I want my children to learn good lessons of value and not the wrong way to react or handle troubles when they watch me as their mom. Father, I pray that I will be a good mom. I ask You to bless me and show me Your favor in this role You have entrusted to me. In Jesus' name, I pray. Amen.

Training My Children

*Train children to live the right way,
and when they are old, they will not stray from it.*

PROVERBS 22:6 NCV

Dear God, You are always so faithful to point me in the right direction in life. Now I am asking You to help me point my children in the right way. I need wisdom in how to raise them to be godly young men and women. As they grow up, I am committed to teaching them Your scriptures. I will teach them the importance of prayer. I will continue to take them to church, showing them the importance of gathering together in community with other believers. These are imperative things for every Christian to learn and put into practice. I pray Your protection over my children as they grow up. I pray that they would never stray from Your side but be faithful to You all the days of their lives. I love the promise I find in Proverbs that says they will not depart from the truth if we train them up in it. I know they may drift off the right path at times; they are human, just as I am. I have certainly made my share of mistakes! But I pray that they would learn to hear Your voice and that it will stand out loud and clear above the other voices that call to them. You are their Good Shepherd. Guide and protect them, Lord. In Jesus' name, I ask these things. Amen.

A Peaceful Home

*My people will live in peaceful places
and in safe homes and in calm places of rest.*

ISAIAH 32:18 NCV

Dear God, make my home a haven for my family and for all who come through its doors. It is so much more than just walls to us. It is where we laugh and cry. It is a shelter from the storms of life. It is where we gather to eat our meals and sleep at night. We work and play here. We want this home to honor You. Father, as we raise our children, I ask a special blessing on this home. I ask that they would know it is a safe place for them. I pray that they would always feel comfortable sharing their burdens with my husband and me. I want them to know they can come to us with anything, that we are always here for them. Even if we don't have answers to their questions or solutions to their problems, we can listen and we can help them. Together, with You in our lives, we can handle anything. Please ensure that our home will always be a place of peace and rest and security. Thank You for our home, and I pray our children feel stable and loved here always. In Jesus' name, I pray. Amen.

Disciplining My Children

*The rod and reproof give wisdom, but a child
left to himself brings shame to his mother.*

PROVERBS 29:15 ESV

Heavenly Father, I want my children to love me. I want them to laugh more than they cry. I want to say yes more than I say no. But I realize that discipline is of great importance. Help me to let go of the desire to be my children's friend or favorite. Help that to be replaced with a righteous desire to raise them appropriately in the ways You have set before me as a mother. My children need limits and boundaries. They need to learn what is right and what is wrong. I am doing them a great disservice if I do not discipline them. If I leave my children to do as they wish, they will be in grave danger—not only physically, but also emotionally and spiritually. Give me direction, Lord. Show me how to discipline them so that their lives will be peaceful and they will stay on the right path. It is in Jesus' name I ask for help in raising my children. Amen.

Raising Godly Children

"You shall teach them to your children, talking of them when you are sitting in your house, and when you are walking by the way, and when you lie down, and when you rise."

DEUTERONOMY 11:19 ESV

God, I am not just a mother. . .I am a teacher. I may not have formal schooling in education, but I am the primary teacher of my children. My husband and I bear great responsibility here. Help us to live up to the roles of godly parents. Every moment is a teachable moment for our kids, Lord. Help us to never take the easy way out. Help us to take the time to instruct our children in Your ways and in Your Word. As we go through our days and nights, may we teach them well. As our children face hardships, help us to speak truth into their lives. As they experience joy, help us to remember to give You all the glory, that they in turn may do likewise. When we gather around our table, may Your Word be read. May Your precepts be discussed. May we teach our children and bring them up in such a way that You are honored greatly through their choices and through their very lives. In Jesus' name, I pray. Amen.

Dedicating Our Children to God

*"For this child I prayed, and the LORD has granted me
my petition that I made to him. Therefore I have lent
him to the LORD. As long as he lives, he is lent to
the LORD." And he worshiped the LORD there.*

1 SAMUEL 1:27–28 ESV

Just as Hannah dedicated Samuel to You, heavenly Father, I
dedicate my children to You. I lift them up to You by name. My
husband and I longed for children. We asked You to bless us
with a family, and You answered our prayers. You have gifted us
with the children You wanted us to have. You have put them in
our care, and now we give them back to You. We will nurture
Your children, Lord. We will care for them. We will teach them
of Your great love and that You created them as unique beings
in Your very image. We will instruct them in the holy scriptures.
We will teach them how to live. We dedicate ourselves—and our
whole family—to You, God. Give us wisdom as we raise these
children. May our home be filled with joy and laughter. May
it reflect the eternal love You have for each of us. May we be a
family known for getting along; and when we are asked what
makes our family different, may our answer always quickly be
"Jesus." In His name, we pray. Amen.

Obedience

Children, obey your parents in
everything, for this pleases the Lord.

COLOSSIANS 3:20 ESV

God, obedience is an issue in our home. I admit it. You see everything, anyway! I can't hide it from You. My children disobey, and we are working on it. I know the importance of teaching them to obey our instructions. If they don't learn to obey their mother and father, how will they ever learn to submit to their heavenly Father? Give us wisdom, Father, in the best ways to teach them and discipline them. We need peace in our household again. There is so much arguing, and it gets so out of hand. Sometimes the struggle is so awful, we just want to give up. We would like to let them do whatever they want! But, my husband and I both know that despite the fact that we have strong-willed kids, we must train them to obey us. We are the authority You have set over them, and teaching them to obey is our job. Father, I pray for peace. I pray for a transformation in my children's hearts. I pray that they will understand that the things we tell them to do are for their own good. Help them know we are on their side. Please help us with the issue of disobedience in our home. We need You, Lord. In Jesus' name, I pray. Amen.

Treasured Time with My Children

But Jesus said, "Let the little children come to me and do not hinder them, for to such belongs the kingdom of heaven."

MATTHEW 19:14 ESV

Father God, give me more time with my children. They are growing up so quickly. Some of my favorite times are right before bed when we read and snuggle together. Help me to make time for this. Show me the importance of gathering my children close. You loved the little children. You rebuked Your disciples when they tried to clear away the crowd of kids. You reached out to children. You held them and spoke with them. You wanted them. You valued them. Remind me each day that these babies You have blessed me with are treasures. They are worth more than any project or deadline. They mean the world to me. Help me to never neglect my time with them. Multiply my time, I pray. I have so much to do; there's no denying there's a lot on my plate. But help me to prioritize so that I always have time for my children. I thank You for my kids, and I pray we will always be close. In Jesus' name, amen.

God, Grant Me Serenity
IN MY FINANCES

Protection from Greed

For the love of money is a root of all kinds of evil.
Some people, eager for money, have wandered from
the faith and pierced themselves with many griefs.

1 TIMOTHY 6:10 NIV

Heavenly Father, thank You for blessing me financially. Thank You for my job and for the ability to pay my bills. Thank You for providing for my family. Help me to always see money as merely a resource and not a treasure to be hoarded. I want to use all of my resources, including my financial resources, for Your kingdom. When I see a need, I want to be free to meet it. Lord, show me opportunities to bless others. Thank You for my church and the blessing of tithing. Through my church, I am able to know that my financial gifts are being used responsibly. I pray that You would always bless this area of my life and remind me to be generous with the resources You give me. Please protect me always from the love of money, which is the root of many evils. I ask this in Jesus' name. Amen.

Guidance in Financial Decisions

*Dishonest money dwindles away, but whoever
gathers money little by little makes it grow.*

PROVERBS 13:11 NIV

God, I know many people who are after the get-rich-quick schemes. They scramble to try to make a fast buck; but in the end, I know it will only lead to destruction and debt. Help me to always be wise in how I make, save, and spend money. Thank You for wise financial advisers who are there to help direct me in my decisions. Thank You for guiding me to the organizations and individuals I should support financially. Father, I ask You to bless me with insights regarding investing. Show me also when I should loosen the purse strings a bit and be more generous. You are the giver of all good gifts. Everything that I have comes from You. Remind me of this and allow me to never hold too tightly to any earthly thing—including money. It is in Jesus' name, I pray. Amen.

Treasures in Heaven

"Do not store up for yourselves treasures on earth, where moths and
vermin destroy, and where thieves break in and steal. But store up
for yourselves treasures in heaven, where moths and vermin do
not destroy, and where thieves do not break in and steal."

MATTHEW 6:19–20 NIV

Heavenly Father, I pray that You would help me keep my priorities straight when it comes to my finances. I could work my life away sticking more money in the bank. I could save it all and hoard it for a rainy day, but that rainy day may never come. I can't take the cash with me to heaven. . .so help me instead to store up treasures in heaven. Help my real investments to be in people and relationships and service. Help my treasures to be time spent and scriptures shared. Help me to focus on heavenly things more than I worry about earthly ones. Bless me in my earthly finances, I pray; but far greater is my desire for Your blessing in the things of value in Your economy. Your economy looks quite different from the one in this crazy, upside-down world in which I live. May my treasures always be stored up in heaven where they will be of eternal value. In Christ's name, I pray. Amen.

The Love of Money

Whoever loves money never has enough; whoever loves wealth is never satisfied with their income. This too is meaningless.

ECCLESIASTES 5:10 NIV

God, I love You. I love Your world and Your people. I love sunsets and sunrises painted by Your hands—masterpieces for Your children to enjoy. I love Your Word, full of wisdom and truth, which teaches and corrects me every day of my life. I love Jesus, who died upon the cross for my sins. I love my family and my friends, people hand chosen by You to enrich my life. I love the seasons of the year and how they remind me that You are always in control and that You are a God of order. But I do not love money. Sure, it can buy things that my family needs. It can sponsor a child who is starving in Africa. It can send a missionary abroad. It can provide a meal in Jesus' name. But it is just a resource—nothing more than a tool. Please help me to never fall in love with money! If a person loves money, he or she always wants more of it. Help me to always be content and thankful for whatever money You bestow upon me. And help me to use it wisely. In Jesus' name, I pray. Amen.

Serve God, Not Money

"No one can serve two masters. Either you will hate the one and love the other, or you will be devoted to the one and despise the other. You cannot serve both God and money."

MATTHEW 6:24 NIV

Heavenly Father, You are my Master. You are my Lord. I want to follow in Your footsteps and walk in Your ways. I see those who chase after money. They have made money their god. They worship it and seek it. They devour it when they find it. And, for them, there is never enough. As they attain money, their hunger for it increases. There is no end to the vicious cycle. When times are good and money is abundant, they are happy. When times are bad and the money is scarce, they fall into depression. If a person's whole world is built upon a foundation of cash and coins, it is certain to crumble. Please help me to always keep my priorities straight when it comes to money. Thank You for Your provision of the money that I need to support my family. Thank You for the deep peace I find in knowing that You are my God and that money is merely a tool You provide. In Jesus' name, I pray. Amen.

An Extravagant Gift

*While Jesus was in Bethany in the home of Simon
the Leper, a woman came to him with an alabaster
jar of very expensive perfume, which she poured
on his head as he was reclining at the table.*

MATTHEW 26:6–7 NIV

Heavenly Father, the disciples saw this woman's gift as a waste. She, who poured expensive perfume on Your head, was expressing her great love for You. She was anointing You with it. She had saved the best for her Lord. And yet, she was scolded for her extravagant gift. But You stopped them. You told Your followers that she had done the right thing. You told them the poor would always be there, but that You were going away soon. How I hope I would have acted as the woman rather than as the disciples! How I hope that my best is always saved for my Master. How I hope that I never hesitate for even a second when there is a gift I possess that could be of use to You, Father! Teach me to hold loosely to money and possessions. They are not what's important in this world. Show me that even though sometimes it might appear more practical to use money in a certain way, You may place a call on me that is unique. Just as this woman poured perfume upon Your head, may I be prepared to give as I am led to do. In Jesus' name, I pray. Amen.

Financial Peace

Do not be one who shakes hands in pledge or puts up
security for debts; if you lack the means to pay,
your very bed will be snatched from under you.

PROVERBS 22:26–27 NIV

Heavenly Father, I pray for guidance in my financial decisions. Give me wisdom, I pray, to know whether to take out a loan, how to pay off a debt quickly, and other matters of money I face daily. God, I know that it is best to keep short tabs. I know that it is best to pay cash. Show me how to operate according to these principles. A debt-free life offers great peace and serenity. Living under the burden of debt is never fun. I know that in Your Word You say the only debt that should remain between two people is the debt of love. I should strive to owe nothing in regard to money. Help me to find ways to become debt free and stay that way so I will be free to be more generous in my giving. Teach me Your principles, Lord. Guide me to wise counsel which can help me get a handle on my finances. I want this area of my life to be aligned with Your statutes. I want to honor You with my finances and find financial peace. In Jesus' name, I pray. Amen.

Debt-Free Living

Let no debt remain outstanding, except
the continuing debt to love one another, for
whoever loves others has fulfilled the law.

ROMANS 13:8 NIV

Heavenly Father, I haven't always been wise with money. I pray that You will guide me and show me ways to allocate my money so that I can pay off debt. I truly want to be debt free so that I may honor You in this area of my life. It seems so hard to live within my means, but I know it can be done if I put my mind to it. It is not good to have debts lingering, hanging over my head. I know that when I rid myself of debt, I will be opening up my world to a new level of peace. All the time I spend worrying about money I can then devote to serving You and showing love to those around me. I will have more money to give to good causes. I will be able to support Your Church better. I pray for guidance that I might get out of debt quickly. Thank You, Father, for hearing my prayer. I know You will help me. In Jesus' name, I pray. Amen.

God, Grant Me Serenity
IN CHANGE

Courage to Face Change

"Be strong and courageous. Do not be afraid or terrified because of them, for the LORD your God goes with you; he will never leave you nor forsake you."

DEUTERONOMY 31:6 NIV

God, change is scary. I was used to the old normal, but now there is a new normal. But it's not quite "normal" to me yet! I pray that I will find courage and strength to face the changes in my life. I need to sense Your nearness at this time. As I step out of my comfort zone, I ask that You would provide a peace that passes all understanding. At times when I feel overwhelmed, I pray You would remind me that transitions require a lot from us. They take time to get used to. Soon I will look back on this change and be able to see the good in it. Change isn't easy, but there are always blessings to be found in it. Just like a child hunting for special pebbles in the schoolyard, guide me to the gems in this transition. Help me to value the new and to loosen my grip on the old just a bit. I want to cherish the memories of what was, while at the same time embracing what has come to be. Thank You for change, Lord, and for walking through it with me. In Jesus' name, I pray. Amen.

A Time for Change

*There is a time for everything, and a season
for every activity under the heavens.*

ECCLESIASTES 3:1 NIV

There is a time for everything, God. You make this so clear in Your Word. This change in my life was not unexpected to You. You had it in Your plans. You knew I would struggle with it, but You also know the outcome. You see a year. . .five years. . .ten years into my future. You know the blessings and benefits of this transition, while I can only see the moment. You see the whole puzzle, each piece locking in and fulfilling its role in the final picture. Help me to remember that there is a time for everything, just as we are taught in Ecclesiastes. You created me. You know the plans You have for me. Every day that I will live has been ordained by You. Bear with me in my weakness, as change is always hard for me, Lord. Bring over me a peace that cannot be explained. Bring rest to my weary soul, and help me—in this moment—to let go of the control. Help me to realize I serve a sovereign God who has not made a mistake, nor has He taken His hand off my life, even for a brief second. You are in this change, Lord. Help me to embrace it. In Jesus' name, I pray. Amen.

Jesus Never Changes

Jesus Christ is the same yesterday and today and forever.
HEBREWS 13:8 NIV

Jesus, You are always the same. You have not changed. When everything around me is altered, You remain. You are steadfast. The same yesterday, today, and tomorrow. You are good. You are above all things and before all things. You hold all things together. Help me to dwell on these truths and to rest in You. I may feel like my world is spinning out of control, but You are right here with me. And You will never let me go. This change in my world does not change who You are, my Savior. In times of insecurity, may I cling to You, my Rock and my Redeemer. You are a mighty fortress. Thank You for helping me to know and understand that You will never change and You will never leave me. I find such comfort in this! I can rest easy in the knowledge that You are still here and You are forever by my side. I surrender all to You, Jesus. This change. This uncertainty. This worry. Help me to adjust well, Father. Help me to release control to You. You are more than capable of handling this for me! In Your name, I pray. Amen.

God Makes a Way

*"See, I am doing a new thing! Now it springs up;
do you not perceive it? I am making a way in the
wilderness and streams in the wasteland."*

ISAIAH 43:19 NIV

Lord, You are a God of the unexpected. You bring about changes we don't count on but that are just right for us. You know us individually. You understand our strengths and weaknesses. You see our needs. You make a way where, frankly, at times there seems to be no way. You create a stream in the wastelands. You clear a path through the wilderness. Although this is uncharted territory for me, You have been here already. You have made Your preparations for me to come to this place in life. You know me, and You know all about this change that has come along. I will walk with You, Father. I will hold on to Your strong hand and let You guide me through this land. I will walk when You say walk, and run when You say run. I believe with all my heart that even if the change feels like a dead end or a wrong turn to me, there is good in it. You know the plans You have for me, and they are always in my best interest. Thank You, God, for always looking out for me. In the name of Christ, I pray. Amen.

Do Not Lose Heart

Therefore we do not lose heart. Though outwardly we are
wasting away, yet inwardly we are being renewed day by day.
For our light and momentary troubles are achieving for us an
eternal glory that far outweighs them all. So we fix our eyes
not on what is seen, but on what is unseen, since what is
seen is temporary, but what is unseen is eternal.

2 Corinthians 4:16–18 niv

God, this change is tough. It feels like I might not make it through. It's overwhelming to me. I feel, at times, that You are requiring too much of me. I have faced transition before, but this time I just don't know that I can make it to the other side. Your Word tells me not to lose heart. Your Word assures me that You are there, right in the midst of this change that seems to be too much for me to handle. Renew me day by day, Lord. Sometimes I need that renewal more often—hour by hour, even moment by moment. I know You are able to help me. I know this struggle is temporary. In time, it will pass. And this change, this transition, this "new" that replaces the familiar—it has a purpose. I can trust that You are not going to waste it in my life. You will use it for my good. Help me not to look at the problem, but rather to look up. Help me to focus on Jesus, who is the same yesterday, today, and forever. In His name, I pray. Amen.

Hope in the Lord

*Yet this I call to mind and therefore I have hope: because of the
LORD's great love we are not consumed, for his compassions never
fail. They are new every morning; great is your faithfulness.*

LAMENTATIONS 3:21–23 NIV

Father God, You are faithful. Through all the changes I must endure, You are true. You do not change like shifting shadows. You remain. You hold on to me. You sing over me as I lay my head on my pillow and trust in You to see me through the night. This time is not easy. I am in new and unfamiliar territory. Everything feels strange. Nothing seems normal anymore. It is a lonely feeling. I miss the old, which has been replaced so suddenly with the new. I read that Your mercies are new every morning. I need them, God. I need to experience Your mercies today—right now, God. I have been so self-reliant in the past, but right now I bow before You in submission. I realize that I can't get through this on my own strength. I need You every hour. Be gracious, Lord. See me through this change as only You can. In Jesus' name, I ask. . .knowing You will provide. Amen.

Blessings in Change

"For my thoughts are not your thoughts, neither are your ways my ways, declares the LORD. For as the heavens are higher than the earth, so are my ways higher than your ways and my thoughts than your thoughts."

ISAIAH 55:8–9 ESV

God, I wasn't expecting to have to face a change like this right now in my life. It's certainly not what I wanted. Help me to rest in the knowledge that this is not a surprise to You. Your ways are higher than mine, and You do have a purpose for this change that has come along. I know this to be true, Father. I felt so solid in my footing. I was plodding along in one direction when suddenly I find myself on a brand-new path. These surroundings are strange to me. The winds of change have taken me to a new place with a new purpose; and honestly, I feel lost. Thank You that You are still on the throne. You are still in control. You have plans for me. And You will bring good from this transition. This change may not be comfortable or easy or even welcomed, but it is going to be okay. Because You are my God, and I trust in Your ways. Your understanding is far greater than mine. In Jesus' name, I commit this change to You. In His name, I pray. Amen.

God, Grant Me Serenity
IN MY CHALLENGES

God Is with Me

"So do not fear, for I am with you; do not be dismayed,
for I am your God. I will strengthen you and help you;
I will uphold you with my righteous right hand."

ISAIAH 41:10 NIV

I am up against a challenge, Father. I feel so small in its shadow. This is one of those times when I want to lean back into Your chest and listen to Your heartbeat. It beats for me, Lord, I know. Like an earthly father who wants nothing more than to protect his children from harm, You long to protect me. You are my God. You have more strength than all the earthly fathers of this world combined. With You, I have no reason to fear. This challenge is great, God. I'm not going to pretend it's not. I feel like it is even greater than me, and it probably is! But it is not greater than You, Father. Strengthen me, I pray. Uphold me. Carry me into battle day by day until we are victorious and this challenge lies flat, like the giant Goliath from young David's perfect aim. It may loom large before me, but this challenge is child's play for You. Let's tackle it together. Bless me with peace and courage as we fight this, Lord. In Jesus' name, I pray. Amen.

Peace in the Face of Struggle

*"I have told you these things, so that in me you may have peace.
In this world you will have trouble. But take heart!
I have overcome the world."*

JOHN 16:33 NIV

Jesus, You are the Prince of Peace. And I need Your peace as I face this struggle. It is greater than me; but I know it has nothing on You! You told me that this world would have trouble. Up to this point, I have not known real trouble. But now it lies across my path like a boulder, and I have no idea how to move it. Whether You remove the trial or lead me through it, I ask for peace along the way. It may take days or weeks or even months. I may still be dealing with this challenge years from now. But I do know that day by day, I can walk in peace, even if this trouble doesn't disappear instantly. You are with me, and You are fully equipped to face the challenges ahead of us. Thank You for always being with me. Thank You for Your assurance. I am so thankful we are in this together. In Jesus' name, amen.

Focused on the Lord

I keep my eyes always on the LORD.
With him at my right hand, I will not be shaken.

PSALM 16:8 NIV

God, I remember the story of Your disciple who set out to walk upon the water. As long as he kept his eyes on You, he walked across the surface of the sea. But when he lost his focus, he began to sink. He had to keep his eyes on You in order to be successful. There is a great lesson for me in this story. I feel like I am in the greatest struggle of my life right now. I must keep my eyes on You. When I stare into the face of this trial, it is too much for me to bear. I cower at its immenseness. But in doing so, I let Satan win. I hear him laughing, jeering on the sidelines, that he knew I would never make it. I hear him chuckle at my insecurities. But then You appear, Father. You reach out to me. You remind me to hold strong to my faith. You assure me that if You could make a man walk upon water, You can smooth this path out before me—and You will. It may take time. But together, we can conquer this. I will keep my eyes on You. I refuse to let Satan win. I will not be shaken. I will rely on You, my God, and in Your strength I will prevail. In the name of Jesus, I pray. Amen.

Casting My Cares on Him

Cast your cares on the LORD and he will sustain you;
he will never let the righteous be shaken.

PSALM 55:22 NIV

Lord, I give You my cares and concerns. I offer this challenge to You as a sacrifice on the altar. I need You to sustain me. I need You to uphold me. I am weary from the struggle; I have no more strength. I am through trying to face this on my own. Will You fight the battle in my place? Will You go before me? Will You defend me on all sides? Will You bring me success? I trust You to see me through, as only You can. I have struck out on my own enough. I should have learned by now that some trials are just too tough for a mere human. There are battles waging for my soul in the spiritual realms. And this is one of them. Fight for me, Jesus. I trust in You. Amen.

Trials Are Gifts

Consider it a sheer gift, friends, when tests and challenges come at you from all sides. You know that under pressure, your faith-life is forced into the open and shows its true colors. So don't try to get out of anything prematurely. Let it do its work so you become mature and well-developed, not deficient in any way.

JAMES 1:2–4 MSG

God, this trial is stronger than I am. It is testing me in ways I have never been tested before. I am challenged at all sides, and I don't know what to do. Strengthen my faith in this time of difficulty, I pray. Walk with me. Take me *through* it, even though it would be so much easier to find a shortcut *around* it. I know that when we come out on the other side of this roadblock, You will have strengthened my faith through the experience. So while I cannot say I am excited about facing it, I will rejoice even in this trial. I know it will be for my good in the long run. Thank You for assuring me that You will be with me. I am ready to tackle this challenge with You—we can do it together! In Jesus' name, I ask for the strength and endurance I know I will need in the days to come. Amen.

Help from the Lord

*If you don't know what you're doing, pray to the Father. He loves
to help. You'll get his help, and won't be condescended to when you
ask for it. Ask boldly, believingly, without a second thought. People
who "worry their prayers" are like wind-whipped waves. Don't
think you're going to get anything from the Master that way,
adrift at sea, keeping all your options open.*

JAMES 1:5–8 MSG

I don't know what I'm doing, Lord. I'm up against a trial that
has me stumped. I have tried every angle and keep coming up
empty. So I come to You. I lay my burden at Your feet because
You care for me. I cast it at the foot of the throne, and I cry out
to You for help. I come before You confidently, not sheepishly.
I am not a stranger to You. I am Your child. I am requesting the
aid of my Creator, my Father, my Redeemer, my best friend. You
are my Abba Father, my Daddy. You are the One who knows
me and sees me. You know the way out of this mess I have gotten
myself entangled in, and I need You to work. Boldly, I pray for
Your assistance. I thank You in advance, because I know that help
is on the way. In Jesus' name, I pray. Amen.

The Lord Fights for Me

The LORD gives me strength and a song. He has saved me. Shouts of joy and victory come from the tents of those who do right: "The LORD has done powerful things." The power of the LORD has won the victory; with his power the LORD has done mighty things.

PSALM 118:14–16 NCV

Heavenly Father, I think of all the trials I have faced. You have walked through them with me—day by day. You have let me lean on You. Some days You have completely carried me. You have made a way for me, and I know You will do the same this time. There are moments when I am so weak that all I can do is speak the name of Jesus. And in those times, I speak it boldly. I cry out to You as I drive in my car, tears streaming down my cheeks. I speak Your name as anxiety overwhelms me. I do not beg it but command it to leave me in the name of Jesus. I walk on. I fight on. When this battle is won, just as others have been, I will praise Your name. I will give You all the glory for seeing me through it. You save me again and again, Father. Often, You are called upon to save me even from myself. And You always show up. You never lose a fight. You are victorious, Lord. I praise You now in advance for the victory I know You will provide in the face of yet another enemy. I am ready to go into battle with You, Father. In Jesus' name, I pray. Amen.

The Lord Answers Me

When I was in trouble, I called
to the LORD, and he answered me.

PSALM 120:1 NCV

Lord, I need You. Just as a little child calls out in the night when she is frightened, I call out to You now. There is so much peace and comfort for me in the knowledge that You are there. You are right by my side the instant that I call to You. You are ready to help me face this giant. You have provided all the tools. I will put on the breastplate of righteousness; I will take up my shield; I will call to mind the promises of Your holy Word that give me assurance I will get through this. Every time I have faced trouble in the past, You have been there. I have erected altars of remembrance. There are so many of them! I am facing yet another battle now. Help me in this trial. Thank You for the peace I feel just knowing we are in this together. I know I never fight alone. In Jesus' name, I pray. Amen.

God, Grant Me Serenity
IN MY DISAPPOINTMENTS

All Things Work Together for Good

*And we know that in all things God
works for the good of those who love him,
who have been called according to his purpose.*

ROMANS 8:28 NIV

Heavenly Father, remind me today that *all things* work together for good in the lives of those who love You. I love how this verse in scripture does not say that *some* things work together for good. It doesn't say *most* things. It says very clearly that *all things* in my life work together for good. This includes my disappointments and my failures. It means that there is not a mistake that You cannot redeem in my life for Your purposes. You are bigger than my mistakes. You are bigger than my dreams that don't come true. You take the broken pieces and the fragments that are left, and You put them together to create a beautiful masterpiece. It may be different from the one I had imagined, but it will be even better! You are a good God, and You have good plans for me. You are using all things together for my good. Thank You for that, Lord. It brings me peace in the midst of disappointment. In Jesus' name, I pray. Amen.

I Will Yet Praise Him

*Why, my soul, are you downcast? Why so disturbed
within me? Put your hope in God, for I will
yet praise him, my Savior and my God.*

PSALM 42:11 NIV

Dear heavenly Father, I am so depressed. What I had hoped for
has not come to pass. My dream is crushed. My heart is broken.
My disappointment wells up inside and shows itself through tears.
I am so distressed. And yet, in moments of clarity, I can see that
even now You are God and You are in control. I will praise You
even now. For You are my Savior. You are my God. You are my
Rock and Redeemer, and You hold all things together. The earth
spins on its axis because You will it to. You have not forgotten
me. My current situation is not a mistake. It is not beyond You,
Father. You are able to do more than I can imagine even in my
wildest dreams. You can take this time of sorrow and use it to grow
a stronger me. New doors will open where old ones have slammed
shut. New opportunities will spring forth in my life. You will
put them there in my path. I trust You, God. Even in this time of
loss and grief for what I thought might be. I give it all to You in
Jesus' name. And I praise You even though I do not understand.
Amen.

God Is Still There

*Whoever dwells in the shelter of the Most High will rest in the
shadow of the Almighty. I will say of the LORD, "He is my refuge
and my fortress, my God, in whom I trust." Surely he will save you
from the fowler's snare and from the deadly pestilence.*

PSALM 91:1–3 NIV

God, I know You haven't left me or even looked away for one
moment. I know You are still here. You are the same yesterday, today, and forever. That brings me great comfort, because
right now I feel like my world has been turned upside down. I
am so disappointed. I am struggling, God. I refuse to crumble
at this trial. I will instead call out to You, my God. I reside in
the shelter of Your presence. I rest now in Your shadow. You
are my refuge, my hiding place, a fortress that protects me. I
will place my trust in You. Certainly You will protect me from
failure. You will raise me up. Lift up my countenance, God.
Set my sights on whatever is next. Take from me my past with
its disappointment, and provide a new dream for me to hold on
to. In Jesus' name, I pray. Amen.

God Hears My Cry for Help

When the righteous cry for help, the LORD hears. . . . The LORD is near to the brokenhearted and saves the crushed in spirit. Many are the afflictions of the righteous, but the LORD delivers him out of them all.

PSALM 34:17–19 ESV

Thank You, heavenly Father, for hearing me when I cry. Things are tough lately, and I am so discouraged. I know that You are near to me. I can sense Your presence throughout my day. I hear You in the encouraging words of Christian brothers and sisters. I see You in nature as the sun continues to rise and set, even when I am so disheartened. You save the crushed in spirit. You deliver Your own out of afflictions. Please see my hurt and heal my brokenness. Put me back together so that once again I can feel whole. I will serve You all of my days. Some days are just harder than others; I struggle to get out of bed and face the world. Help me today, Lord. Give me strength. Remind me that even in my distress, You have not forgotten me. You will see me through, and even this shall pass. In Jesus' name, I pray. Amen.

Discouraged, but Not in Despair

We are hard pressed on every side, but not crushed; perplexed,
but not in despair; persecuted, but not abandoned;
struck down, but not destroyed.

2 CORINTHIANS 4:8–9 NIV

Heavenly Father, thank You for being my Rock. You are there, and I instantly turn to You when I am in distress. I may be hard-pressed on all sides, feeling the weight of the world on my shoulders, but I am not crushed. You reach down and help me carry the load. You will never give me more than I can bear. I am confused; I don't understand why things have ended up as they have. I never wanted to face this type of disappointment; but even in this confusion, I refuse to give up. I will not despair even in my disappointment. I will stand strong in my faith. I will trust in You. I may face persecution, but I will never be abandoned. I may fall down, but I will get up again in Your strength. I am not destroyed. I may have some battle scars, but I will be victorious. I have Christ in my heart, and I can do all things through Him who strengthens me. In His name, I pray. Amen.

Walk by Faith

For we walk by faith, not by sight.

2 CORINTHIANS 5:7 ESV

Dear Jesus, I will walk by faith through this disappointment. I will face this difficulty head-on and won't back down. I will remember all You have shown me in the light while I walk through the darkness. You have revealed to me that You are the Son of God. You are the Messiah sent to save us from our sins. You promise us abundant life here on earth and eternal life with You in heaven when we die. I have much to look forward to! Even so, right now I am disappointed. I am hurt. I am somewhat disheartened, Lord. You see that, and You understand. You understand that I am human. You experienced every human emotion when You walked this earth. You were fully man but also fully God. You were tempted. You experienced disappointment. You were betrayed by those You held closest in Your inner circle. Thank You, Lord Jesus, that I do not walk alone. Thank You that I do not walk only according to what I can see, because frankly, at times I can't see more than one step ahead. Give me the grace to walk in the light that I have been given for this day. Help me, Jesus, to walk by faith. In Your name, I pray. Amen.

Nothing Shall Separate Me from God

What then shall we say to these things? If God is for us, who can be against us? He who did not spare his own Son but gave him up for us all, how will he not also with him graciously give us all things? Who shall bring any charge against God's elect? It is God who justifies. Who is to condemn? Christ Jesus is the one who died— more than that, who was raised—who is at the right hand of God, who indeed is interceding for us. Who shall separate us from the love of Christ? Shall tribulation, or distress, or persecution, or famine, or nakedness, or danger, or sword?

ROMANS 8:31–35 ESV

God, I am thankful for the peace I have in You. I am comforted when I read in Your Word that You will never leave me. If You are for me, it doesn't matter who else is against me. You are the God of the universe, and You are on my side. You are my Father. When I look up, You are always there to guide me and protect me along the way. If You sacrificed Your only Son to die for my sins, would You withhold anything from me? Certainly not! You are the Giver of all good gifts. In my disappointment, I recognize that what seems to have gone all wrong may instead be just right in Your plan book. You have good plans for me. Tribulation will not do me in. Distress is not my endgame. I am a winner because I am on Your team. In Jesus' name, I pray. Amen.

Resist the Devil

Be sober-minded; be watchful. Your adversary the devil prowls around like a roaring lion, seeking someone to devour.

1 PETER 5:8 ESV

Heavenly Father, I pray that I would not let the devil have a foothold in this situation. I am struggling, but I am not destroyed. I will not fall prey to the evil one, who would love to see me give up on You. I find my hope in the living God. Satan would love for me to believe that this is the end of the road, that I should just give up. In him there is no hope; but in my God, there is *always* hope. Satan wants to tear me apart and devour me. He is like a lion in the jungle, just ready to pounce on its prey. Keep me ever watchful. Make me aware of his sneaky schemes. When I hear a message in my mind that tells me I am not strong enough, help me to stop right then and take that thought captive to Jesus. I am strong enough—not in and of myself—but through Christ, who gives me strength. I pray, in Jesus' name, against the schemes of the evil one. Amen.

Everlasting God

Have you not known? Have you not heard? The LORD is the everlasting God, the Creator of the ends of the earth. He does not faint or grow weary; his understanding is unsearchable. He gives power to the faint, and to him who has no might he increases strength. Even youths shall faint and be weary, and young men shall fall exhausted; but they who wait for the LORD shall renew their strength; they shall mount up with wings like eagles; they shall run and not be weary; they shall walk and not faint.

ISAIAH 40:28–31 ESV

God, You never grow weary. I am so tired of being tired. You are the Creator. I am merely the created. You never run out of power. I am spent. You are strong. I am weak. The good news for me is that I have chosen to wait upon the Lord. In this time of disappointment and heartache, I cry out to You. I remember Your promises. I stand on them. I draw upon Your strength. I am renewed by Your everlasting power. I may be only the created, but I am made in the image of my Creator. I bear Your signature as Your created masterpiece. Even on my darkest day, this little light of mine still shines. Today I need Your strength, Father. I cannot do life on my own. Remind me of that timeless truth, that forever promise that I will run and not grow weary, I will walk and not faint. Help me to mount up with wings like eagles and soar. In Jesus' name, I pray. Amen.

God, Grant Me Serenity
WITH MY PAST

God Restores the Years Eaten by Locusts

"I will restore to you the years that the swarming locust has eaten, the hopper, the destroyer, and the cutter, my great army, which I sent among you."

JOEL 2:25 ESV

God, I've wasted a lot of years. I wish I could get them back. I was not who I should've been. I wasn't walking with You. It pains me to think of all that wasted time. Time I could have spent in Your Word. Time I could have spent serving You. I feel behind in my study of the Bible when I compare myself to others my age. I think of all those whom I could have led to Christ, but I was squandering away my time on useless pursuits instead. But You assure me that You will restore those years to me. With You, nothing is wasted. You are the Redeemer. You redeem my past. You use it. You set before me opportunities to share my testimony. You may use my story to alter the story of another person, Father. You may use my past to save someone from walking down the same roads that lead to nowhere. God, You are the restorer of wasted things. You bring beauty from ashes. In Jesus' name, I commit my past to You, asking You to redeem it. Amen.

God's Mercies Are New Every Day

I will sing of your strength, in the morning I will sing of your love;
for you are my fortress, my refuge in times of trouble.

PSALM 59:16 NIV

God, Your mercies are new every morning. I haven't made the best decisions in the past, and it has caused me some heartache, but today is a new day. Each day You give me a clean slate. I wake up singing of Your love. It envelops me and reminds me that I am not the sum of what I have done. I am saved by the blood of Jesus. I am not my past; I am Your child. My past mistakes do not define me. I am ready to begin anew. You are my fortress. You take care of me in times of trouble. When I am tempted to return to my old ways, You remind me of the blessings of walking with You. When I turn to look over my shoulder, You take my hand and lead me forward into the bright future You have planned for me. Because of You, Father, my future will be better than my past. Jesus makes all the difference in the world. In His name, I pray. Amen.

Forgetting the Past

*Brothers and sisters, I do not consider myself yet to have taken hold
of it. But one thing I do: Forgetting what is behind and straining
toward what is ahead, I press on toward the goal to win the prize
for which God has called me heavenward in Christ Jesus.*

PHILIPPIANS 3:13–14 NIV

Heavenly Father, I can relate to the apostle Paul. I started out
on a really bad track but have seen the light. I am walking with
Jesus; and while my past really stinks, I still have a bright future
ahead of me. Help me, God, to truly forget what is behind and
strain toward what is ahead. It's hard to close the door on what
has happened in the past. It seeps back into my memories and
sometimes in my dreams. I try to take every thought captive to
Christ, but some days it is easier to do than others. As I seek to
press on toward the goal, remind me daily that You are with me.
I need You by my side in order to truly lay aside the negative
and run toward the positive. I am so blessed in my new life to be
walking with Jesus. Please help me to never return to my old sin
nature. In Jesus' name, I pray. Amen.

New Life in Christ

"I have been crucified with Christ and I no longer live,
but Christ lives in me. The life I now live in the body, I live
by faith in the Son of God, who loved me and gave himself
for me. I do not set aside the grace of God, for if righteousness
could be gained through the law, Christ died for nothing!"

GALATIANS 2:20–21 NIV

Dear God, it's truly a miracle. New life. I have been born again. Nicodemus didn't understand this concept. He thought Jesus meant that a man would truly be born of his mother's womb a second time. However, I understand the concept, and even beyond that, I have experienced it. A spiritual rebirth. A second chance. A new lease on life. I thank You that my old life died and that I was raised to a new life. The old me is now dead. It was put to death when I accepted Jesus. And just as Jesus rose from the dead after three days in the grave, I stand here a new woman. I will live by faith in Christ, who made this new life possible for me. I recognize that I am not saved by works but by grace and that I cannot boast in my salvation. I owe it all to Christ. In His precious name, I pray. Amen.

He Forgets My Past Sin

Do not remember the sins of my youth and my rebellious ways;
according to your love remember me, for you, LORD, are good.

PSALM 25:7 NIV

Dear heavenly Father, I know that You tell me You have forgotten my sin. So why do I keep reminding You of it? You tell me that You have cast it as far as the east is from the west. And yet, I feel the pangs of guilt almost every day. I see the consequences of my past sin; I am living out those consequences. I know that things would be different had I made better choices. But I hear You whisper over me that You will work all things together for good. You can create beauty from messes. You did it in the life of Saul, who became Paul. You used tax collectors and prostitutes for Your purposes, Father God. You see us as righteous once we are saved. You see me through a Jesus lens. Everything that was in my past, You have graciously left there. Now help me to do the same so that I may find peace, Father. I ask that You would remind me of Your goodness and of Your unfailing love for me. In Jesus' name, I pray. Amen.

Live in the Present

*The LORD says, "Forget what happened before,
and do not think about the past."*

ISAIAH 43:18 NCV

Lord, I can't stop living in the past. I dig up old memories, and they drag me down. I heard once that if you live in the past, you will miss the present; and therefore, you will have no future. I think this is true. I am seeing it played out in my life. I am afraid to take risks, Lord. I fear being hurt, so I refuse to let down the walls I have constructed around my heart. Each time I get close to someone, I pull away. I look back over my shoulder. I wonder if this person will leave me. I wonder if I will regret trusting him or her. I question everything in my present experience because of my past. God, I need this to change. I want to enjoy today. You have placed blessings and opportunities in my life, and You want me to fully live. But I can't fully live until I lay down the past. Will You help me? Will You show me how? I am Your child, and You are my Father. I trust that You will guide me. Show me the right people to talk to if I need godly counsel. Take me to the place of healing, whether it is through counseling or writing a letter to someone from my past. . .or whatever path You see fit. I love You, Father, and I thank You for helping me to find peace with my past. In Jesus' name, I pray. Amen.

Blessings of the Present

Don't ask, "Why was life better in the 'good old days'?"
It is not wise to ask such questions.

ECCLESIASTES 7:10 NCV

God, I remember the words to an old song: "Count your blessings. Name them one by one. Count your blessings. See what God has done. Count your blessings. Count your blessings. Count your many blessings. See what God has done!" Sometimes I forget to do this. I look back on the past, and I have such fond memories. I dwell there when I should live in the present. Regardless of how great the past was, there were issues and struggles there also. We often look back with rose-colored glasses, remembering what we want to remember. Every season has its joys and its sorrows. There is not one that is better than another. Times are different. One season of life may bring more trials than another, but in every season, You are with me. You know the plans You have for me. You use the circumstances I find myself in to teach me and use me and grow me. I am blessed, Father. Thank You for my memories. Some of them are so sweet. But please help me move forward. I don't want to dwell in the past and miss what You have for me today. In Jesus' name, I pray. Amen.

Maturing in Faith

*When I was a child, I talked like a child, I thought
like a child, I reasoned like a child. When I became
a man, I stopped those childish ways.*

1 Corinthians 13:11 NCV

Heavenly Father, You have prepared me for this time. This is my time. Each day that I live is ordained by You. You decided when I was to be born, and You led me to Jesus at just the right time. You opened my eyes spiritually. You saved me. As I live out this life, I pray that my faith will grow. I am more mature in my walk with You now than I was in the past. I pray that I will show that maturity in the ways I serve You and reach out to others. I am not a baby Christian any longer. It is time for me to step up and stop only taking it in and start sharing more of myself with others. Show me opportunities to teach or lead or use my spiritual gifts. I want to honor You in all I do. In the past, I was soaking up Bible knowledge, but I do not want to just "sit and get" all of my life. I am ready to serve. Show me how You want to use me, Lord. In Jesus' name, I pray. Amen.

God, Grant Me Serenity
IN MY GRIEF

No More Tears

"He will wipe away every tear from their eyes,
and there will be no more death, sadness, crying,
or pain, because all the old ways are gone."

REVELATION 21:4 NCV

Heavenly Father, I have experienced a deep loss. The grief overwhelms me. And yet it comes in waves. There are moments when it doesn't completely consume me. Just as the ocean tide ebbs and flows, so it is with grief. In moments of clarity, I remember Your promise that grief is just part of the human experience. The loved ones who go to heaven before us are not mourning. The ones left behind are the ones who grieve. My beloved ones are in a much better place. They are with You now. One day I will go to heaven. I will enter paradise where there are no more tears. There is no such thing as grief where You are, Father. There is no disease or pain. There is no cancer. There are no hospitals or surgeries, because everyone in heaven is given a new body that has been made perfect. On my darkest days when grief will not let up, I rest in the knowledge that one day everything will be made right. I look forward to that, God. I find peace in knowing this life is not all there is for me. One day there will truly be no more tears. In Jesus' name, I pray. Amen.

Comfort in the Lord

"Blessed are those who mourn,
for they shall be comforted."

MATTHEW 5:4 ESV

God of all comfort, I come before You grief-stricken. My heart hurts. I need You to reach down and fill me with supernatural peace. I don't understand this loss. How could it be? And yet, each day I awake to find that it was not a nightmare. This person I loved is really gone. Father, I call out to You. I ache from head to toe. I never knew grief could be so physical. I am physically sick over this loss. I find comfort when I read in Your Word that those who mourn are blessed, for they shall be comforted. As I speak the name of Jesus, I feel You near. I rest in the shadow of Your wing. I don't have the energy to question or even to cry any longer. I just rest here with You. I just allow You to hold me. I take in the comfort and the peace of knowing You. How could anyone face grief without You, Lord? How could anyone make it through a deep loss if there were not the hope of heaven on the other side? I love You, Lord. Thank You for comforting me in my time of grief. In Jesus' name, I pray. Amen.

The Dead in Christ Shall Rise

*But we do not want you to be uninformed, brothers, about those
who are asleep, that you may not grieve as others do who have
no hope. For since we believe that Jesus died and rose again, even
so, through Jesus, God will bring with him those who have fallen
asleep. For this we declare to you by a word from the Lord, that
we who are alive, who are left until the coming of the Lord, will
not precede those who have fallen asleep. For the Lord himself will
descend from heaven with a cry of command, with the voice of an
archangel, and with the sound of the trumpet of God. And the dead
in Christ will rise first. Then we who are alive, who are left, will
be caught up together with them in the clouds to meet the Lord
in the air, and so we will always be with the Lord.*

1 Thessalonians 4:13–17 esv

Heavenly Father, the promises in Your Word are clear. Heaven is
real, and believers in Christ will spend eternity there. It sounds
like a scene from a movie, Father, with awesome special effects.
And yet, it is in Your Word. And it is true! I cannot imagine how
it will feel when that trumpet sounds. To see the dead in Christ
alive again and meeting Jesus in the sky! And then just to be swept
away into the clouds to meet Him! God, it gives me hope in my
time of grief. It gives me joy in my sorrow. I am sad because I
miss my loved one, but I trust that one day all believers will be
reunited for a great big family reunion in the sky. And it will last
for all eternity! In Jesus' name, I pray. Amen.

Jesus Destroyed Death

But it is now shown to us by the coming of our Savior Christ Jesus.
He destroyed death, and through the Good News he showed
us the way to have life that cannot be destroyed.

2 TIMOTHY 1:10 NCV

Heavenly Father, I am so thankful that Jesus defeated death. The sting of death has no more power in the life of a Christian. When death comes, we simply pass over into eternity with You in heaven. We trade a human existence for a spiritual one in paradise. Grief is for those left behind, because we miss our loved ones. But for our loved ones who have passed and know Jesus, there is no more pain for them. There is only victory. There is only joy. They have a new body that is so different from the earthly one they left behind. Father, Jesus has made a way for me to have an abundant life here on earth, and I thank You that He has also gone to prepare a place for me in heaven. I look forward to the glory of heaven. The hope of heaven eases the pain of grief. Find me here in my grief, Father. For even though I know the promises, I am hurting. Sing over me. Comfort me. Help me, Lord, as I walk through sorrow. In Jesus' name, I pray. Amen.

Comforting Others Who Grieve

Blessed be the God and Father of our Lord Jesus Christ, the Father of mercies and God of all comfort, who comforts us in all our affliction, so that we may be able to comfort those who are in any affliction, with the comfort with which we ourselves are comforted by God. For as we share abundantly in Christ's sufferings, so through Christ we share abundantly in comfort too. If we are afflicted, it is for your comfort and salvation; and if we are comforted, it is for your comfort, which you experience when you patiently endure the same sufferings that we suffer. Our hope for you is unshaken, for we know that as you share in our sufferings, you will also share in our comfort.

2 CORINTHIANS 1:3–7 ESV

God, help me to comfort those who grieve. I have been there. I have felt the numbness and the shock of loss. I have been shaken by grief. Remind me that the greatest comfort I can offer comes not through words but through showing up and just being there. Sometimes words sting. They fill up empty space with an attempt to ease the grief, but they sometimes make things worse. Please use me to be a hug or a shoulder to cry on as needed. Please show me tangible ways to help. Blessed are those who mourn. They shall be comforted. Help me to be part of that comfort, Lord. In Jesus' name, I pray. Amen.

God Cares When I Grieve

You have kept count of my tossings; put my tears
in your bottle. Are they not in your book?

PSALM 56:8 ESV

Abba Father, Daddy, You catch my tears. You save them in a bottle. You care. Each tear I cry hurts You. Your heart is a Father's heart, tender toward Your child. You do not wish to see Your daughter in anguish. I cry my eyes out, but in the end, I feel better. Tears sometimes help in a strange sort of way. They bring a release to my sorrow. They cleanse my soul and allow me to move forward. I think tears can be healthy at times. Thank You for creating emotions, Father. Keeping our feelings inside is never good. God, I love You and I thank You for caring for me. Help me to cast this grief at the foot of Your throne. Help me to trade my burden for Yours, which is lighter. I surrender my grief to You. In Jesus' name, I pray. Amen.

In Christ, I Can Do All Things

I can do all things through him who strengthens me.

PHILIPPIANS 4:13 ESV

I can do all things, Lord, through You. You strengthen me. You lift me up when I feel I can't go on. Where I see only one set of footprints in the sand, as the poem goes, it is then that You are carrying me. How I need You to carry me today. Grief zaps my energy. I find it hard to concentrate. My mind drifts. My heart aches. Every little thing around me reminds me of the past and of my loved one who has passed. I must rely on Your strength, for I truly have no resources of my own. Because Christ lives in my heart, I can press on. I will lie down and rest in peace; and when I awake, I will find enough power to face another day. I will take it one day at a time. I know that in due time I will be stronger and back to my old self. I love You, Lord, and I thank You for strengthening me in times like this. In Jesus' name, I pray. Amen.

Jesus Heals

He heals the brokenhearted and binds up their wounds.

PSALM 147:3 ESV

My heart is broken, Lord. I have lost someone so dear to me. My heart wells up with grief, and I can think of nothing else. Nothing seems right in the world now. There is a huge void that no one else will ever be able to fill. I am so sad. In these quiet moments with You, I find comfort in Your Word. I read that You heal the brokenhearted. Could this mean that You can heal me? Can You take the broken pieces of my heart and somehow put them together again? I know that life will never be the same. I know that I will have to create a new normal. But I find peace in knowing that You heal those whose hearts are broken, because that is my condition in this grief. Bind up my wounds, Lord Jesus. Nurse me back to a place of mental, emotional, and physical health. This grief has affected every aspect of my life. Take care of me. I am usually the caregiver, looking out for those around me. I don't have the strength to take care of others right now, Father. I need You in these days. I need You every hour. Be merciful with me, I pray. Thank You for the comfort of knowing You care and that You promise to take care of me. In Your name, I pray. Amen.

God, Grant Me Serenity
IN MY FAITH

Faith

Now faith is the assurance of things hoped for,
the conviction of things not seen.

HEBREWS 11:1 ESV

God, this world focuses on things that can be seen. Money, fashion, entertainment. The spiritual realm is much the opposite. I must learn to focus on what is unseen—this is faith. Faith is the assurance of things hoped for. It is a promise that there is more to this life than meets the eye. It is trusting that the sun will rise tomorrow if You will it to, Father. It is recognizing that I serve a God far bigger than myself, far grander than the boundaries of this world. You are able to work miracles. You are capable of far more than we can even imagine. Strengthen my faith, I pray. In times when I have only a tiny mustard seed of faith, I pray You would bless that offering of trust and grow it in Jesus' name. Amen.

Mustard Seed Faith

He said to them, "Because of your little faith. For truly,
I say to you, if you have faith like a grain of mustard seed,
you will say to this mountain, 'Move from here to there,'
and it will move, and nothing will be impossible for you."

MATTHEW 17:20 ESV

God, I want to come before You with great faith. I want to be like those listed in the Bible's roll call of faith. I want to be like Noah, who worked on the ark when he could not see the rain. I want to be like Abraham, who climbed the mountain, knife in hand, ready to sacrifice his beloved son if You asked him to. I want to please You with my faith the way the great men and women of the Bible did. But I keep coming up short. I have but a mustard seed portion of faith to bring to You. I ask You to multiply it. I ask You to grow it. You tell me in Your Word that I can do great things with even a small amount of faith. I trust this to be true, but I ask You to make me a woman of greater faith. In Jesus' name, I pray. Amen.

God's Word Grows My Faith

All Scripture is breathed out by God and profitable for teaching,
for reproof, for correction, and for training in righteousness,
that the man of God may be complete, equipped for every good work.

2 TIMOTHY 3:16–17 ESV

God, thank You for Your Word. All scripture is breathed by You. It teaches me. I benefit from reading it. The words jump off the pages. They correct me when I am wrong. They train me in righteousness so that I might know the right roads to take and the right decisions to make. I want to honor You in all I do. God, I am confident that as I study Your Word, my faith will grow. I will be competent to serve You, using my gifts for Your glory. I am equipped for good works through the reading of Your Word. When I do these good deeds, others will see them. They will wonder what makes me tick. They will ask me why I care as I do, why I serve, why I minister to others in their times of need. The answer will always be simply "Jesus." My good deeds can point others to Him. Bless me, Father, as I seek to grow in my faith. I want to honor You in my circumstances. Use me, I pray, in Jesus' name. Amen.

Faith in God, Not Man

*That your faith might not rest in the wisdom
of men but in the power of God.*

1 CORINTHIANS 2:5 ESV

God, I am often tempted to place my faith in man instead of where it belongs—in You. I trust in those around me and almost make them my gods at times. Certainly I want to please my employer, but he or she is not my God. Certainly I hope I can trust friends and family members, but my ultimate trust must be in my Lord. Give me discernment, Father, to see when I am trusting too greatly in man and not enough in You. I love You, Lord, and I have placed my faith in You. I am saved by grace through faith in Jesus, and I want to have a greater, stronger faith. You have come through for me again and again. Teach me to build altars at these places where You have blessed me. I want to live by faith, knowing that You will always come through for me. In Jesus' name, I pray. Amen.

Faith and Works

But someone will say, "You have faith and I have works.
Show me your faith apart from your works, and I will
show you my faith by my works.

JAMES 2:18 ESV

God, I show my faith through my works. The two go hand in hand. I cannot say I have faith and then just sit there and not do anything about it. Help me to never live in such a hypocritical manner. I find great peace when I am living out my faith. It requires something of me. It requires sacrifice. But it is a wonderful kind of tired when I grow tired from serving. Allow me to see the opportunities set before me to do good works. I will share my faith with those around me, and I will be faithful to You, Lord. Even when I am not faithful, You remain the same. Draw me close and teach me how to have more faith each day of my life. I love You. In Jesus' name, I pray. Amen.

Faith in Jesus

"Truly, truly, I say to you,
whoever believes has eternal life."

JOHN 6:47 ESV

Heavenly Father, so many people say they "believe," but they don't believe in You. Some have faith in themselves. They believe that they are strong. They don't see that they are weak and that only through You are they able to be strengthened. Some believe in many gods. These are lowercase *g* gods. They are not gods at all, in reality. Some believe in people. They make movie stars and employers and boyfriends their gods. They seek approval from these people. They long to be like them. They follow hard after empty pursuits. God, I am so thankful that the object of my faith is Jesus Christ. He died upon the cross for me—a horrible death. He bore my sins and the sins of the whole world that day. He opened up a path for me to come before You, a holy God. He is the way, the truth, and the life. No one comes to the Father but through Jesus. Thank You for my faith that promises me eternal life. In Jesus' name, I pray. Amen.

God Is Faithful

*But he was in the stern, asleep on the cushion. And they woke him
and said to him, "Teacher, do you not care that we are perishing?"
And he awoke and rebuked the wind and said to the sea, "Peace!
Be still!" And the wind ceased, and there was a great calm. He said
to them, "Why are you so afraid? Have you still no faith?" And they
were filled with great fear and said to one another, "Who then is
this, that even the wind and the sea obey him?"*

MARK 4:38–41 ESV

Heavenly Father, I am not so unlike the disciples, am I? I know
You as the One who rebuked the sea, and yet I do not trust
You to calm the storms in my life. I have an advantage over the
disciples. I can read the scriptures and learn of all the times You
proved Yourself powerful. I watch the Red Sea's waters part. I see
Noah and his family saved from the flood inside the giant ark. I
hear the baby's cry—a baby born to old parents, Abraham and
Sarah. A promise fulfilled. You are faithful. You have great power.
I know this. And yet, I still doubt. Give me greater faith, I pray.
In times when I rely on my faith, I feel such peace. I am comforted
to know I serve a God who always comes through. You will calm
the storms in my life, or You will carry me through them. Either
way, You are faithful. In Jesus' name, I pray. Amen.

God, Grant Me Serenity
IN MY CIRCUMSTANCES

Remain Faithful to God Regardless of Circumstances

*"If you throw us into the blazing furnace, the God we serve is able
to save us from the furnace. He will save us from your power,
O king. But even if God does not save us, we want you,
O king, to know this: We will not serve your gods
or worship the gold statue you have set up."*

DANIEL 3:17–18 NCV

Heavenly Father, Daniel and his friends were bold in negative circumstances. The king was totally against them. He tried to get them to worship a gold statue instead of You, the one true God. The king threatened to throw them into the blazing furnace. Even so, these men did not cower. They stood firm in their faith. They told the king that regardless of their circumstances, they would not bow to another god. They would worship You. They trusted You to save them from the fiery furnace; but they said that they would remain faithful to You even if You didn't. They still would not bow to the gold statue. They would have no other god before You. They would not let their circumstances dictate their faithfulness. Let it be so of me. May I be found loyal to You, Lord, regardless of what comes my way. In Jesus' name, I pray. Amen.

Love God

*And he answered, "You shall love the Lord your God with all your
heart and with all your soul and with all your strength and
with all your mind, and your neighbor as yourself."*

LUKE 10:27 ESV

God, regardless of my circumstances, I am called to love You
with all my heart, soul, strength, and mind. I am called to love
my neighbor as myself. So in times of rejoicing and victory, Lord,
I will love You. And in times of want, I will love You just as
much. I don't want my faith to be swayed by the winds of change.
No matter where I find myself, may I always be found faithful.
Help me not to focus on the outward circumstances, but instead
help me see You in everything. When I am hurt, I have the op-
portunity to draw close to You and let You comfort me. When I
am praised by others, I get to point them to my Lord. Regardless of my situation, may my love for You be evident to all those
who know me. I love You, God. In Jesus' name, I pray. Amen.

Serenity in Suffering

This is what you were called to do, because Christ
suffered for you and gave you an example
to follow. So you should do as he did.

1 PETER 2:21 NCV

Jesus, You suffered. You were persecuted. You were betrayed. You hung on a cross between two thieves to die a painful death. You had done nothing wrong to deserve crucifixion, and yet You hung there for me. You suffered in my place. And now I am called to suffer. I will follow Your example. I will suffer as You did. I will not run from it. I will face it head-on. If the cup shall not pass, I will drink deep of suffering. If suffering is God's will for me, I will try to endure it without complaining. I am not promised a carefree life. I am promised trouble in this life, because it is a fallen world since sin entered in. The good news is that You have overcome this world, Father. There is life beyond earth. There is hope beyond suffering. This is not the end but only the beginning. Allow me to suffer graciously. Allow me to rise above my circumstances. In Jesus' name, I ask for serenity even in suffering. Amen.

God Will Show Up

But as for me, I am poor and needy;
may the Lord think of me. You are my help
and my deliverer; you are my God, do not delay.

PSALM 40:17 NIV

God, You are never too early, and You are never too late. My circumstances are not great right now. I find myself in need. I have met with times that I never knew would come. I lived in plenty, but now I know what it means to live in want. I don't know where the money will come from and how the bills will be paid. The mortgage is due. The bills stack up. I need Your help in these times. I need to be delivered by Your hand. Provide for me, I pray. Remember my family, I ask. I know that You are aware of our needs. Please show up at just the right time. Please alter our circumstances. Do not delay. So many times in the past, I have needed You in other ways. I need You to show up again, God. You are greater than these circumstances. You are stronger. You are higher. In the power of Jesus' name, I pray. Amen.

Peace in Any Circumstance

*Great peace have those who love your law,
and nothing can make them stumble.*

PSALM 119:165 NIV

Heavenly Father, I love You. I love Your Word. It is a light unto my path. It sheds light into the dark recesses of my mind. It gives instruction and correction. It comforts and guides. I love Your law. I seek to obey Your commands and walk in Your ways. I know that when I do so, my life is filled with peace, regardless of my outward circumstances. You have not promised that I won't get cancer. You do not say I am immune to grief. Quite the opposite! You assure me that in this world I will find trouble. But I will continue to love You. I will continue to read and meditate upon Your law. I will walk in Your ways and seek to do Your will all the days of my life. Nothing can make me stumble if this is true. Nothing. No illness. No sorrow. No disappointment or loss. No set of circumstances has the power to steal my joy unless I allow it. I choose joy. I choose Jesus. I choose life. In the name of Christ, I pray. Amen.

The Promise of Eternity

"I know that my redeemer lives, and that in the end he will stand on
the earth. And after my skin has been destroyed, yet in my flesh
I will see God; I myself will see him with my own eyes—
I, and not another. How my heart yearns within me!"

JOB 19:25–27 NIV

God, Job was a faithful servant. He endured so many trials and tribulations, but he remained true to his faith. I don't know how he did it, but I pray for faith like Job's. I pray that in any circumstance, I will remain true to You. Regardless of how bad it gets, I have the hope of heaven. I have the hope of life beyond this earth. This is a fallen world. Ever since Adam and Eve sinned in the garden and death entered into the equation, there has been suffering. There has been disease and loss and sorrow. No matter what comes to me, I will be okay. I have a Redeemer who lives. I have a promise that Jesus is coming back, and He will gather His own to Himself. I have the promise of eternity. So if disease should steal my health or mental well-being or strength, I will cling to my faith. I know that Jesus lives and that I will spend eternity with Him. In His name, I pray. Amen.

Focus on Jesus

*You will keep in perfect peace those whose
minds are steadfast, because they trust in you.*

ISAIAH 26:3 NIV

God of peace, meet me here. I am weary from my day, and I do not see relief in sight. This situation has exhausted me. I am tired, but I am not defeated. I find rest in You. I find comfort in knowing that You are God. Just as a little child never takes her eyes off her parent while she plays nearby on the playground, I will fix my eyes on You. I know that You are mine and that I am Yours. I belong to You. You guide my steps. You know me, and You desire that I know You. I will read Your Word, and I will meet with You in prayer. I will not do all the talking, because You have designed prayer as a two-way conversation. I will be still and know that You are God. I will listen for You in those moments. I will focus on Your ways. I know that there is great peace to be found for those whose hearts are steadfast. I desire such peace. In Jesus' name, I pray. Amen.

God, Grant Me Serenity
IN MY ASPIRATIONS

Like a River

Good leadership is a channel of water controlled by GOD;
he directs it to whatever ends he chooses.

PROVERBS 21:1 MSG

God, I really have no idea where I am going. The future is very unclear to me. I take solace in the fact that You are in control. I want to be a channel of water controlled by You. Direct the flow. Lead me where You want me to go. Use me as You use a river, Lord. Use me to nourish and to strengthen others. Use me to help them move from one place to another. Use me to provide refreshment to their souls. God, channel me in the right way. Use my strengths and weaknesses and even my dreams in the way You can be glorified best. I want to be a leader that pleases You, one who is at Your disposal to do Your will all the days of my life. Thank You, heavenly Father, that I don't need to have the future all mapped out. It is good to be flexible and to be clay in the Potter's hands. I am ready to be used as You determine best. I commit my future to You. I hold loosely to any aspirations I may have, because the dreams You have for me are far greater than any human mind could conceive! In Jesus' name, I pray. Amen.

Committing My Work to God

Commit your work to the LORD,
and your plans will be established.

PROVERBS 16:3 ESV

God, I commit my work to You. I have so many goals, but I know that none of them can be reached in my own strength. If You are not in my plans, my plans have no point. I ask You to take the goals that I have designed and the dreams in my mind and alter them to conform to Your will. Establish my plans, Father. Bless my hard work. May I find favor with You. Will You help me find favor with my superiors? In my work, Lord, there are so many ladders to climb. There are so many ways to get to the top. I don't desire the easy way. I will take no shortcuts that require me to be unethical. I believe that slow and steady wins the race. I believe that doing things the right way always pays off. I believe that if I commit my aspirations to You, You will bless them. In Jesus' name, I ask You to bless my work and help me to reach my goals if it is Your will. Amen.

Blessed, and a Blessing

Now the LORD said to Abram, "Go from your country and your
kindred and your father's house to the land that I will show you.
And I will make of you a great nation, and I will bless you and
make your name great, so that you will be a blessing. I will bless
those who bless you, and him who dishonors you I will curse,
and in you all the families of the earth shall be blessed."

GENESIS 12:1–3 ESV

God of Abraham, Isaac, and Jacob. . .God of my forefathers. . .
God, who is with me, who made me, who sees me, who longs to
bless me. I come before You. I ask You to bless me and to help
me be a blessing to others. If You allow me to climb the ladder
of success, may I always look for someone I can bring along with
me. May my eyes be ever fixed on You. May I use any position
of authority to bring glory to Your name. May my superiors see
Jesus in me. May I be a difference maker. May those beneath me
see Jesus in me. May they sense it in the way I lead. May I stand
out as a servant leader, one who is never too high up to take on a
menial task. May I look like Jesus in my workplace. I pray that if
You raise me up, I will always remember the One who took me
there. You alone deserve all honor and glory and praise. In Jesus'
name, I pray. Amen.

God Can Do Anything

Now to him who is able to do far more abundantly than all that
we ask or think, according to the power at work within us.

EPHESIANS 3:20 ESV

God, You have great plans for me. They are greater than my wildest dreams or my highest aspirations. Please help me to continue to work hard and set goals. Give me motivation to succeed and to grow. I have so many dreams for my life that I hope to see come true. But remind me that it is not "me, myself, and I" who makes my dreams come true. It is all because of You. You know the plans You have for me, plans to bring me hope and a future. You don't make plans to harm me. So if some of my dreams don't come true, help me to look for the silver lining in the cloud. Help me to look for Your purpose even in the times You say no instead of yes. Like any good parent, You will not let me have something that You know may not be best for me. In Jesus' name, I pray. Amen.

God Establishes My Steps

In their hearts humans plan their course,
but the LORD establishes their steps.

PROVERBS 16:9 NIV

Heavenly Father, I have made my plans. I have set my goals. I know the direction I see myself going in my family life and my career. I recognize my gifts and abilities, and I have ideas of how to best use them for Your glory. But, that being said, I want to submit to Your will. Just as a student submits a draft to her writing teacher but realizes she must be open to the revisions of her instructor, so I submit my plans to You. Mark them up with a red pen, Father. Change the theme. Alter the sequence. Change the direction of it altogether. You are the Master Planner. You are the One who establishes my steps regardless of the dreams I may have. Thank You, God, that I can trust You. You will never take me down a road that is not best for me. You know the plans You have for me, and they are for my good. I find great serenity in the knowledge that You, my God, are in control. In Jesus' name, I pray. Amen.

Grow My Faith

*I am sure of this, that he who began a good work in you
will bring it to completion at the day of Jesus Christ.*

PHILIPPIANS 1:6 ESV

Heavenly Father, You have brought me so far. You have saved me
from my sins. You have written my name in the Lamb's book of
life. You have grown me in my faith. You have provided so many
wonderful opportunities for me. I have made some goals for my
life. I want to know if they are the right ones. I want to continue
to grow in my faith and to mature. I want to please You in all that
I do. If my aspirations do not line up with Your good will for me,
please change my dreams. Please plant in my heart the goals and
desires that You want me to have. Make me open to whatever
You have planned for me. I know that, far more important than
exactly what career path I take, is the way You desire to mature
me in my faith. Use me, God. Alter my dreams as You see fit. In
Jesus' name, I pray. Amen.

If the Lord Wills

Come now, you who say, "Today or tomorrow we will go into such
and such a town and spend a year there and trade and make a
profit"—yet you do not know what tomorrow will bring. What is
your life? For you are a mist that appears for a little time and then
vanishes. Instead you ought to say, "If the Lord wills, we will
live and do this or that." As it is, you boast in your arrogance.
All such boasting is evil. So whoever knows the right
thing to do and fails to do it, for him it is sin.

JAMES 4:13–17 ESV

Heavenly Father, I do not know what tomorrow will bring. I can't
see the future. This doesn't frighten me, though, because I know
the One who holds tomorrow in His hands. Who am I to make
plans? You are God. My life came from dust. I was created in
Your image, but I am far beneath You. I see only this moment and
not one second beyond it. You see all eternity. You are the Alpha
and the Omega. The Beginning and the End. You were before all
things, You are in all things, and You hold all things together. You
never change. I ask You to remind me that all my plans should
be filtered through Your loving fingers. I only desire Your will,
Father. If my dreams are outside of that, I pray You would reveal
that to me. In Jesus' name, I pray. Amen.

Praying for God's Will

*"Your kingdom come, your will be done,
on earth as it is in heaven."*

MATTHEW 6:10 ESV

Lord, Your name is holy, and Your ways are great. I come before You and pray as Jesus taught. I ask that You come quickly. This earth is not my home. But in the meantime, would You use me here? I want to be right in the center of Your will. I want to be Your good and faithful servant. I want my dreams to be Your dreams. What breaks Your heart should break mine. I want to carry out Your will on this earth, whatever that may mean. Reveal to me the needs in the world. Show me how my life can make a difference here. I love You, Father, and I am so thankful that I get to be a small part of what You want to do in this world. In Jesus' name, I pray for Your will to be done in my life. Amen.

God, Grant Me Serenity
WHEN I AM ALONE

Family and Friends

God sets the lonely in families, he leads out the prisoners with singing; but the rebellious live in a sun-scorched land.

PSALM 68:6 NIV

God, sometimes I feel lonely. Thank You for my family members who always have a way of lifting my spirits. Thank You also for friends who have become like family over the years. This world can be a cruel place. There are so many demands on me, and I feel stressed at times. But when I enter into a time of fellowship with my family and friends, all of that seems to disappear. You set the lonely in families. Thank You for the serenity I find when I am surrounded by my loved ones. Help me to be aware of those in my circles who may not have friends and family. Especially at the holidays, Lord, help me to be mindful of those who may experience loneliness. May there always be room in my home for one more to join us! In Jesus' name, I pray. Amen.

Serenity in Solitude

Jesus often withdrew to lonely places and prayed.

LUKE 5:16 NIV

When I am lonely, Lord, I look to You. I find moments of solitude to worship and to pray. Jesus withdrew from the crowds that followed Him. He found "lonely" places. He sought them out. Teach me to do the same. While it is fun to be surrounded by friends, family, and colleagues, I need time to be alone as well. We all do. It is a time to recharge and rejuvenate. I need that downtime. With all the pressures of daily life and all the roles I balance as a woman, this is especially important. Whether it is a few moments I steal to myself before everyone else in the house is awake in the morning or a few moments before bedtime, I pray I will find quiet time each day with You. This is important to my spirit and to my growth as a believer. Give me time to reflect and draw close to You. Show me that it is important for me to sometimes be alone and read Your Word. There is serenity to be found in solitude. In Jesus' name, I pray. Amen.

The Christian Is Never Alone

Turn to me and be gracious to me,
for I am lonely and afflicted.

PSALM 25:16 NIV

Father God, I feel lonely. I need Your comfort and Your companionship. I love that because I am Your child, I never have to truly be alone. It would be frightening to do this life all alone. Instead, I have You near—always. You are at my side. You fight a spiritual battle for my soul in unseen realms. You keep me from falling into the devil's traps. You uphold me with Your righteous right hand. All the days of my life I will have a friend. My Redeemer is not dead in the grave. He is very much alive. I think of those who worship idols. How sad it must be to pray to a statue rather than to a living being, a deity who came down to earth to become a man and dwell among His people. You are the one true God, and I am so thankful that I never have to be alone. In Jesus' name, I pray. Amen.

The Lord Keeps Me Safe

*In peace I will lie down and sleep, for you alone,
Lord, make me dwell in safety.*

PSALM 4:8 NIV

You alone, Lord, are my safety. You are my portion. You are my God. I can find peace even if I am all alone because You are always with me. There is serenity to be found in being a believer in Christ. It is not known by the world. It is a peace that is foreign to the unbeliever. You protect me while I sleep. You set Your angels to guard me throughout my days. I have nothing to fear. Nothing touches my life that is not filtered first through Your fingers. You cause me to dwell in safety. You look out for me. Just as a famous person or a leader of a country walks always with a bodyguard at his side, I walk with my God. You are never far away. You neither sleep nor slumber. All the days of my life I will walk with goodness and mercy following me, because I belong to the Good Shepherd, the Great I Am, the sovereign God of the universe. I am never truly alone because You are with me. I find great peace in this. In Jesus' name, I pray. Amen.

Choose Friends Wisely

One who has unreliable friends soon comes to ruin,
but there is a friend who sticks closer than a brother.

PROVERBS 18:24 NIV

Lord, I don't need a lot of friends. I need a few who stick close and love me well. I look to Your example in this. When You were on earth, You walked closely with the Twelve. They were Your disciples. They followed You. You chose them carefully from among the crowd. You called them out of their families and careers, and they followed You with wild abandon. They knew You were special. They didn't question it. Their allegiance was with You, Jesus. Sometimes I look around and wish I had a lot of friends. I see people who seem to be so popular. Popular is not normally the way of the Christian though. I can keep from being lonely by finding even one friend who sticks closer than a brother. Thank You for friendships like that. Thank You for blessing me with a few just as You had a few. I can love the world and be in it, but not of it. I don't have to be the center of attention or have a crowd of people around at all times in order to feel okay about myself. My security is not found in numbers. My security can only be found in You. Thank You for a close friend who loves me well. Help me to always have such a friend. In Jesus' name, I pray. Amen.

God Sees the Lonely

A father to the fatherless, a defender of widows, is God in his holy dwelling. God sets the lonely in families, he leads out the prisoners with singing; but the rebellious live in a sun-scorched land.

PSALM 68:5–6 NIV

Heavenly Father, You are so aware of our needs. You do not sit on Your throne in heaven and forget about Your children. Your eyes wander to and fro across the land. You see the widow who has lost her husband. You comfort her in her time of grief. You fill up her loneliness. You meet her needs. God, You see the orphan. You comfort him or her. You are a parent to those with no parent. You defend their causes. You fight for those who need someone to fight for them. You are sovereign and holy, and yet You are a God who reaches down to the lowliest of the lowly. Your own Son was born in a stable, laid in a manger for a bed. There was no room for Him in the inn. The world despised and rejected Him. They didn't recognize Him. But You saw Him. You didn't leave Him. When the time was right, He was lifted up. He returned to heaven and sits at Your right hand. You are a father to the fatherless, a defender of widows. You see us in our loneliness. Be with me now, I pray. Comfort me. Provide relationships for me that will fill up my lonely heart. I am often lonely, sometimes even in a crowd. Please bring serenity to my solitude, I pray. In Jesus' name, amen.

God, Grant Me Serenity
In My Pursuit of Wisdom

Peace in Wisdom

Blessed is the one who finds wisdom, and the one who gets understanding, for the gain from her is better than gain from silver and her profit better than gold. She is more precious than jewels, and nothing you desire can compare with her. Long life is in her right hand; in her left hand are riches and honor. Her ways are ways of pleasantness, and all her paths are peace.

Proverbs 3:13–17 ESV

God, I long for wisdom. I seek it and find it when I ask You to bless me with it. I know that it is better to find wisdom than to possess great riches. It is more precious than the finest of jewels. Nothing I desire compares with my desire for wisdom. I think, above all, I long for peace in my life. I have learned that there is sometimes peace even when I am not happy. The two do not necessarily go hand in hand. When I make a decision based on Your statutes and ways, I feel peaceful. I can lay my head on my pillow at night knowing I have chosen wisely. I have honored You. Even if my choice was not popular in the world's eyes, even if I am misunderstood, I have peace. Thank You for the peace that I find in wisdom. Thank You for blessing me with wisdom when I ask You for it with my whole heart. In Jesus' name, I pray. Amen.

Wisdom from Above

But the wisdom from above is first pure,
then peaceable, gentle, open to reason, full of
mercy and good fruits, impartial and sincere.

JAMES 3:17 ESV

Your wisdom is true wisdom, God. So many people scurry around here on earth. They think they have found the keys to success. They promise the same success to others. If you just buy this product . . . If you just take this class. . . If you just become part of this program. . . But these are empty pursuits. They lead to nowhere fast. Your wisdom shines. It stands out. It is different. It is pure. There is no hint of the world in the wisdom that flows down from heaven. It is gentle and open to reason. It is not hotheaded or puffed up with pride. Wisdom is full of mercy and good fruits. It is not all about self. It is not a get-rich-quick scheme or a product that enhances beauty. It is impartial and sincere. There is nothing false or misleading in true wisdom. Give me discernment, Father, as I seek wisdom. Help me to find the peace that comes with wisdom from above. In Jesus' name, I pray for wisdom. Amen.

Standing Out as One Who Is Wise

*Who is like the wise? And who knows the interpretation
of a thing? A man's wisdom makes his face shine,
and the hardness of his face is changed.*

ECCLESIASTES 8:1 ESV

God, I want to stand out as a woman full of Your wisdom. There are people who have walked with You for a long time. I see them in my church and in my community, and I recognize them as Your saints. I see it in their eyes. They are not quick to make snap judgments. They are peaceful people, always ready to listen. They often listen more than they talk, but when they do share some advice, it is always very evidently godly advice. They are slow to speak, but their words bear great weight with those who will listen. God, I want to grow in wisdom. Please give me wisdom from above. Give me insight. Show me Your perspectives. Let me see people and events around me through Your lens rather than my own, which is so limited. In Jesus' name, I ask for wisdom. Amen.

Avoiding Foolishness

One who is wise is cautious and turns away from evil,
but a fool is reckless and careless.

PROVERBS 14:16 ESV

Heavenly Father, make me wise. Give me a cautious spirit that recognizes the evil one. Help me to avoid the pitfalls Satan would love for me to fall into. Help me to be careful and to have wise judgment. There is more at stake than just my own life and my own welfare. The next generation watches me every day. They hear the words that spill from my lips. They take in my reactions to everyday life events. They will follow in my footsteps wherever I may lead them. My children will look a lot like me one day. Please keep me from being reckless and careless. Set a guard over my tongue that I might not sin in my anger. Keep my words pleasing to You. May my conversations be honorable and my word choice pure. Father, always set before me a glimpse into the future. Please bless me with the serenity found in wise choices. I pray these things in the name of the wisest one, Jesus. Amen.

Christ Alone

See to it that no one takes you captive by philosophy and empty deceit, according to human tradition, according to the elemental spirits of the world, and not according to Christ.

COLOSSIANS 2:8 ESV

God, please help me to be strong. There are so many voices calling out to me, offering their own brands of wisdom. There are other religions that seem similar to Christianity; help me to discern the differences. Help me to see the emptiness of the promises of other gods. Some worship idols, statues created by human hands. What could a statue possibly offer me that my God has not already blessed me with? There is no life in the lifeless. Many people live by what their parents have taught them, whether it is right or wrong. They go along with traditions. They go through the motions of ceremonies and act as if it matters, when in the end, they are not changed at all on the inside. It is all outward. Just a show. Just a ritual repeated again and again. There is no wisdom in such activities. Father, may I always follow Christ and Christ alone. Let no one take me captive by philosophy or empty deceit. I do not wish to be entangled in human tradition or a new age movement. I will seek You and You alone. Please bless my life with wisdom and a calm assurance that is found only in following hard after Christ. It is in the name of Jesus, I ask these things. Amen.

Do Not Brag in Wisdom

GOD's Message:

"Don't let the wise brag of their wisdom.
Don't let heroes brag of their exploits.
Don't let the rich brag of their riches.
If you brag, brag of this and this only:
That you understand and know me.
I'm GOD, and I act in loyal love.
I do what's right and set things right and fair,
and delight in those who do the same things.
These are my trademarks."

JEREMIAH 9:23–24 MSG

Lord, thank You that I can know You. While I don't know You fully, I am seeking to know You more each day. I study Your scriptures. I fellowship with Your people. I listen to my pastor and other church leaders. I seek wisdom, and I recognize that it is only found in You. Father, may I never brag about any wisdom that I gain, for it is all a gift from You. It comes straight from Your hand. May I boast only in You. You are good. You are loyal, and You act in love. You do what is right. You set things straight. One day every knee shall bow and every tongue confess that You are Lord. Until then, may I delight in the bits of wisdom You graciously bestow upon me. May I seek to be a bit more like You each day. The way of wisdom brings with it a refreshment to the soul. In Jesus' name, I pray. Amen.

Walking with the Wise

*Walk with the wise and become wise, for a companion
of fools suffers harm. Trouble pursues the sinner, but the
righteous are rewarded with good things. A good person
leaves an inheritance for their children's children, but a
sinner's wealth is stored up for the righteous.*

PROVERBS 13:20–22 NIV

God, thank You for wise friends. Thank You for the relatives I have
in my life who pursue wisdom and walk closely with You. Thank
You for the Christian leaders in my circle. They lead me well in
the way of wisdom. Father, I know that I could so easily be swept
into friendships and acquaintances that would lead me down
the wrong paths. I have tasted of the world's brand of wisdom,
and I want nothing of it ever again. Please provide for me wise
and godly companions to do life with. There is something to be
said for a community of believers with older members who can
guide the younger ones. I look to these gray-headed saints. They
have gained wisdom in their many years of walking with You.
Please allow me to walk with the wise so that I might also become
wise. Provide godly counsel at times when it is needed in my
life. Thank You for the peace that comes through walking with
those who walk with You. In Jesus' name, I pray. Amen.

Fear of the Lord Is the Beginning of Wisdom

Give instruction to a wise man, and he will be still wiser; teach a righteous man, and he will increase in learning. The fear of the LORD is the beginning of wisdom, and the knowledge of the Holy One is insight. For by me your days will be multiplied, and years will be added to your life. If you are wise, you are wise for yourself; if you scoff, you alone will bear it.

PROVERBS 9:9–12 ESV

Lord, I have a healthy fear of You. It is not a fear that shudders in Your presence or cowers when You draw near. You are a God of love, and I am Your beloved child. But I have a fear of You, just the same. It is a respect. It is a reverence. You are not my buddy that I might come before You playfully or in jest. I do not treat You as a brother or sister. You are my heavenly Father. I come before You with respect. The beginning of wisdom is the fear of the Lord. Please bless me with wisdom, God. I long to know You better. I believe there is so much for me to learn. Give me insight as I read Your Word. Help me to read, not as one who wears spiritual blinders, but as one enlightened by my God. In Jesus' name, I ask these things. Amen.

Scripture Index